BY J. MARK BAKER

Contents

Introduction 2

Weeks 1–40 4-83

Acknowledgments 84

About the Author... 84

About the Online Audio....................................... 84

To access audio, visit:
www.halleonard.com/mylibrary

Cover Illustration by Birck Cox

ISBN 978-1-5400-6287-1

HAL•LEONARD®

Copyright © 2021 by HAL LEONARD LLC
International Copyright Secured   All Rights Reserved

No part of this publication may be reproduced in any form or by any means
without the prior written permission of the Publisher.

Visit Hal Leonard Online at
www.halleonard.com

Contact us:
Hal Leonard
7777 West Bluemound Road
Milwaukee, WI 53213
Email: info@halleonard.com

In Europe, contact:
Hal Leonard Europe Limited
42 Wigmore Street
Marylebone, London, W1U 2RN
Email: info@halleonardeurope.com

In Australia, contact:
Hal Leonard Australia Pty. Ltd.
4 Lentara Court
Cheltenham, Victoria, 3192 Australia
Email: info@halleonard.com.au

INTRODUCTION

Posture

The voice is unique in that your instrument is really your whole body—not just your vocal cords. And whereas, if playing a wind or stringed instrument, one must learn how to hold it properly, for singing, we must make sure our bodies are properly aligned. That means we always need to observe good posture, whether we are standing or sitting.

Flutists and violinists, for example, often stand when practicing. If they're playing in an orchestra, however, they typically are seated. Similarly, singers usually vocalize while standing, but are often seated during the course of a workaday choir rehearsal.

As singers, our standing posture should be well-aligned, but never stiff. Place your feet apart, about shoulder width. You'll maintain your balance more easily if you place one foot slightly forward. Imagine there's a marionette string attached to the top of your head and another one attached to the base of your sternum. Those strings will allow you to "lean up" gently, rather than to assume a rigid military-like stance.

When sitting to sing, unless you're using a specially designed choral chair that immediately puts you in a good posture, avoid making contact with the seatback. Sit tall, but lean forward slightly; that way, you have easy access to your breathing muscles. "Sit on your feet, not on your seat" is a maxim most choral singers have heard many times. In other words, keep both feet on the floor and allow them to help you maintain a good balance. Never cross your legs nor lean against the seatback in a reclining position.

Always keep your shoulders relaxed. You never want them to become tense or to "ride up" as you sing. This is the sort of unhealthy muscle tension that can too easily transfer itself to your neck and impede free and easy singing. Additionally, make sure your head is well aligned with your body: your chin should neither jut out nor be tucked down.

Breathing

Now that you are in a good, relaxed, well-aligned posture, let's focus on breathing. It's amazing how many singers—even established professionals—sometimes lack good breath management and the proper support of the voice it provides.

If you are completely new to singing, it may surprise you to learn that your chest muscles have little-to-nothing to do with proper breathing. "But wait. Aren't my lungs in my chest?" Yes, but it is your abdominal muscles and back muscles that facilitate good breath management. While it's true the intercostal muscles (the ones between your ribs) expand/contract slightly during inhalation/exhalation, their role is actually a passive one.

Your diaphragm is another important element in the breathing apparatus. It is a muscle that is located horizontally between your chest cavity (thorax) and your abdomen (epigastrium). As noted earlier, in diaphragmatic breathing, your belly expands to pull air into the lungs. Your chest should not rise.

Singing with an open throat

It probably would surprise you—and me!—to learn just how many "career" singers never discovered nor utilized the concept of an open throat. The easiest way to contrast the physical sensation of a closed throat versus an open one is to compare the feeling of swallowing with the feeling of yawning. Try it.

Swallow. Notice your larynx ("voice box") goes up in your throat, your tongue goes back in your throat, your soft palate comes down and closes off your nasal passages, and the walls of your throat close in.

Now yawn. It's the polar opposite, isn't it? Your larynx moves down, your tongue comes out of your throat, your soft palate stretches up and back, and the walls of your throat relax and open. These are the sensations you want to hardwire into your muscle memory!

Onsets in singing

How you begin a note or phrase—the very first sound you make—is called the onset. Voice teachers often use three main terms to label these: 1) glottal; 2) aspirated; 3) balanced. It's the latter that we generally want to aim for. Let's define these.

A glottal onset can sound pushed or hard, because the vocal cords are too closed. Say, very precisely, "I ate an apple." Did you hear and feel what happened at the beginning of each word? That sensation is sometimes called a "glottal stop," because your glottis closed and stopped the air to articulate the vowel sound that began each word. Now say, "Hi hate han happle." Notice how breathy that sounded? That's the aspirated onset. Your cords were not closed enough and you might even have run out of breath. In a balanced onset, the vocal cords are closed, but not too much. It produces a free, easy sound that is neither too constricted nor too loose. Take a breath and sing *oo*, being careful not to begin with a glottal stop. That's the sensation of the balanced onset.

Resonance

When singers and voice teachers speak of resonance, they're taking about singing with spaciousness and a full tone. Without resonance, our singing sounds thin and weak, more like children than adults. So how do we make resonance happen? By creating open space—giving the sound a place to blossom—and by a well-regulated flow of breath.

There are three chambers, so to speak, where the voice resonates: 1) the pharynx; 2) the mouth; 3) the nasal cavities. Let's discuss these separately. The pharynx is the space behind your mouth that extends up into your nasal cavity and down into your throat. It is the primary resonator. The mouth, obviously, is where we shape vowels and articulate consonants to produce words. We want an open throat (like a yawn) and a raised soft palate (like saying "ah" at the doctor's office). The jaw should be relaxed when it opens, not forced too wide and never jutting outward.

Though the nasal cavity participates in resonance, we never—unless we're singing for a comic effect—want the sound to be "nasally." The chief cause of nasality is a lowered soft palate. The "pinch test" is an effective way to make sure your soft palate is raised when singing vowels: Sing a vowel and pinch your nose. If an unpleasant nasal sound occurs, your palate is down; if no change occurs, your palate is raised. That's what you want!

Vocal registration

Vocal registration is a term that is borrowed from pipe-organ playing. The various registers (or stops) are controlled by pulling knobs that control the "on" and "off" position for that particular set of pipes. (That's where the term "pulling out all the stops" comes from; it means using all the organ's musical forces.) By using various combinations of pipes, the organist is able to create a palette of tonal colors appropriate to various styles of music.

Similarly, the human voice has registers with discernably different tone colors. Depending on the voice teachers you ask, or the vocal pedagogy books you read, or the websites you access, you will get a variety of opinions about the matter. In truth, adult singers have only two vocal registers: head voice (often called "falsetto" when referring to men's use of it) and chest voice. All of us have experienced these. Women tend naturally to sing in head voice, though pop singers and Broadway "belters" may use more chest voice. Men tend naturally to sing in chest voice, though the classically trained countertenor and certain pop groups (Bee Gees, for example) may use more head voice. Some pedagogues include mixed voice as a third register, but it is just that: a mixture of head voice and chest voice, not a separate entity.

The challenge, in building our voices and increasing their range of notes and tone colors, is crossing the break—which occurs, in all voices, from about D to F above middle C. The tried-and-true way is to develop the head and chest registers separately and, over time, combine them together into a seamless whole.

Vowels

In singing, vowels are used not only to communicate the words, but also to create a space where the vocal sound can resonate. We classify vowels as open or closed, depending upon the relative size of the mouth opening. Additionally, we classify them as front or back. Say "mee-mah" slowly. Can you feel intuitively that *ee* is a closed front vowel and that *ah* is an open back vowel?

Now say, slowly, "mee-may-mih-meh." Likewise, speak "noo-noh-naw-nah." In both instances, you moved from closed to open. The latter set used back vowels, while the first used front and medial vowels. In the course of this book, we will explore each of these vowel spectrums.

We also classify vowels as primary (fundamental) and secondary (subordinate). The vowels *ee*, *eh*, *ah*, *aw*, and *oo* are primary; all others are secondary.

How to use this book

Vocal Aerobics is a versatile tool that can be used in any number of ways, depending upon your personal objectives. If you are new to singing and are ready to start from the beginning, treat the book much as you would an instruction manual for any topic: Start at the very beginning—it's a very good place to start—and work your way through it, day by day and week by week.

It is important to review and sing exercises you have already mastered. Start your daily regimen with simpler patterns, and in your middle range. Warm up the middle voice before moving to the extremes, especially the higher extremes.

If you have been singing for a bit longer, or even quite some time, and are looking to increase your range, your endurance, your agility, and your musicality, you likewise could take the day-by-approach, or just seek out the exercises that focus on your prescribed goal. Likewise, this book is a treasure trove for voice teachers looking for vocalises to assign their students and for choir directors in need of new choral warm-ups.

VOCAL AEROBICS — WEEK 1

MON

Topic: Breathing

Our first exercise allows you to get a slow-motion sense of how breathing works. Avoiding muscle tension, purse your lips into a straw-sized opening—or use an actual straw (an eco-friendly one, of course) if you prefer. Empty your lungs of air, then fill them slowly while sipping on your faux/real straw. What you should feel is the expansion of your abdominals (yes, your belly should be bigger) as well as an expansion of your lower back muscles (if you want to get technical, these are called *latissimus dorsi*). You can monitor this with both hands, one on your belly and the other on your lower back.

Now that your lungs are full, reverse the process by hissing out. Place your tongue behind your upper front teeth and send the air out through that small aperture. The sound should be that of a prolonged *s*. Now the abdominal and back muscles are going to operate in the opposite direction, contracting to force the oxygen out. When you've contracted your stomach muscles as much as you can, your lungs should be fairly empty. Stop. Never press down with your chest muscles in an effort to empty the last few cubic centimeters (CCs) of air.

(musical notation: sip — hiss — sip — hiss, repeated on two lines)

TUE

Topic: Breathing

Of course, when we're singing a song, we don't have time for really slow inhalation. The same muscles do the work, but much quicker. Your throat should be open and your larynx ("voice box") should lower, the way it does when you yawn. There should be no audible "gasp" when you inhale. If you hear such a sound, it means something is impeding the flow of air into your lungs.

Exhalation, however, is relatively slow, much like the outward hiss. The vocal cords provide gentle resistance, as the outgoing air causes them to vibrate. Before we engage our vocal cords, though, let's practice a one-beat inhalation, followed by a rhythmic hiss. Pulse the eighth notes on beats 1 and 2, and give an extra push of breath through beat 3, releasing on beat 4. Listen to the online demo, then try it yourself.

WED

Topic: Phonation

Now we're going to engage our vocal cords, using the same rhythm as the previous exercise. Use a continuant *n* sound by placing the tip of your tongue just behind your upper front teeth (incisors). On the quarter rest, let your tongue return to its usual resting place as you inhale. Listen to the online demo track before you start.

Tip: For the *n* sound, your tongue is pressed against your hard palate; it's the upper part of your mouth that can't move. Behind it is the soft palate, which is quite malleable and places a big role in shaping vocal sounds and colors. We'll encounter these terms later in the book.

THU

Topic: Phonation

Because muscle memory plays such a big role in singing, it's difficult to correct bad vocal habits once they are ingrained. That's why we're still taking baby steps, to ensure that everything is operating properly. That said, let's keep the same pattern as yesterday's exercise, but sing *mee* instead of the *n*. Make sure the initial *m* sound is well-tuned, placed accurately on the same note as the *ee* vowel.

FRI

Topic: Yawn-sigh, descending

Here's a great technique to begin (and end) your daily vocal warm-ups. Voice teachers refer to it as a yawn-sigh, because that's really what it is! Play a note on your keyboard or pitch pipe, open your throat as you would when yawning. Do you feel the back of your tongue descending? Your larynx (voice box) should also lower itself. Now slide slowly down from the given pitch—all the way to the bottom of your vocal range. Listen to the demo, which covers an octave.

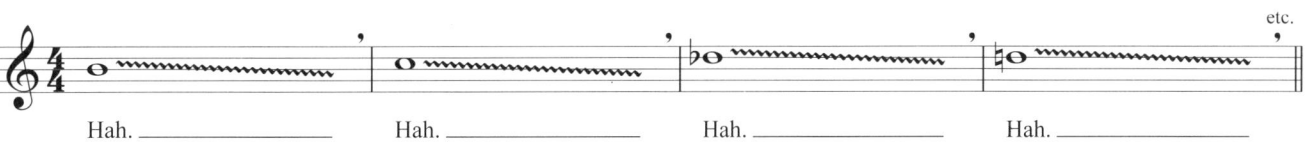

SAT

Topics: Chest voice; AH vowel

This aerobic is especially effective in strengthening your chest voice, so after using it to warm up your middle range, move downward by half steps until your reach your very lowest note. Use a full-on engagement of your vocal cords, but never push past a beautiful sound. (Sing a comfortable mezzo-forte/forte.) Only your tongue should move—not your jaw—quickly transitioning from a closed, front vowel (*ee*) an open, back vowel (*ah*): *ee-ah*, *ee-ah*, *ee-ah*, *ee-ah*, *ee-ah*. The goal is to keep the focus of the *ee* vowel in the *ah* vowel. Monitor your chin with your index finger to make sure it remains still. (That little dash under the quarter notes is called a *tenuto*. It's a reminder to give the note its full value.) Listen to the demo track before you begin.

SUN

Topics: Breathing; abdominal/back muscles; phonation; balanced onset

This simple aerobic will allow us to get our breath moving and our vocal cords vibrating, exercise our back and abdominal muscles, and practice a balanced onset. Inhale on every eighth-rest, just refueling the tiny bit of air you exhaled on the sung notes. The initial *h* will get the breath going. Make sure the *ah* is both spacious and well-focused.

VOCAL AEROBICS — WEEK 2

MON
Topic: Breathing

Today's breathing aerobic expands on an exercise from Week 1 to give the abdominal muscles, back muscles, and diaphragm a good warm-up. We're pulsing eighth notes, and breathing on the rests. Here, we're practicing two different kinds of consonants: voiced and voiceless. In the first four bars, we use only our articulators (lips, teeth, tongue, hard palate); the vocal cords do not participate. In the last four bars, we need to engage the cords as well as the articulators. Listen to the demo before you start.

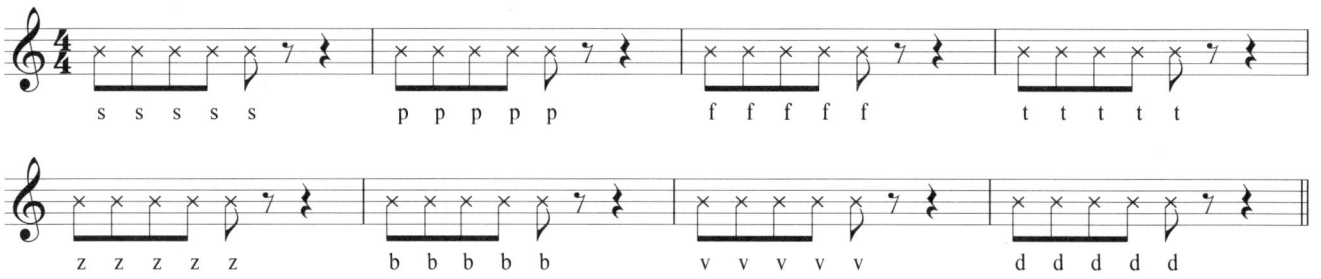

Further practice: Use this exercise two different ways: 1) keep the abdominal muscles moving inward until you reach the rests; 2) allow your belly to expand after each eighth note; go much slower and be careful not to hyperventilate.

TUE
Topic: Intervals

As you work through this book, you'll encounter the term "interval" from time to time. An interval is the distance from one note to another note, ascending or descending. For the most part, the intervals in these exercises will be diatonic—in other words, part of the scale. Below is a brief introduction to the diatonic intervals within an octave. Listen to the demo track, then sing them yourself.

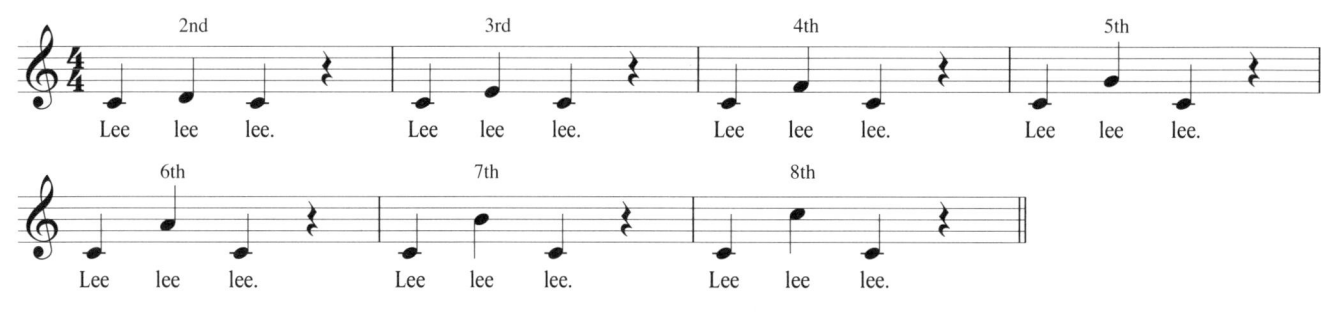

WED
Topic: EE vowel

In the Introduction to this book, we spoke briefly about vowels. (See page 3.) We're going to spend time practicing these and examining what gives each its distinct quality and tone color. Let's begin with the *ee* vowel, which we have already classified as a closed front vowel. The tip of your tongue should touch the back of your lower front teeth, while the front of your tongue arches toward the roof of your mouth. Your jaw should (always!) be relaxed as your lips and teeth assume a smiling position. (Suggestion: Use a mirror to see what this—and future sounds—looks like.)

THU

Topic: IH vowel

The *ih* vowel is slightly more open than the *ee* vowel. The tip of your tongue is forward, and the front of your tongue is raised, though not as high as for *ee*. Raise your upper lip into a smiling position. *Ih* and *ee* are the only two front vowels that are closed.

FRI

Topic: EE vs. IH

Too often, singers fail to make a clear distinction between the *ee* and *ih* sounds. Thus, "*Fill* my heart with joy" becomes "*Feel* my heart, with joy." Those two messages are quite disparate! Practice the sets of words below. Refer to the earlier descriptions of these vowels if you need to—and use your mirror!

SAT

Topic: EH vowel

Eh is an open front vowel. It is not as hard to sing as some try to make it. Simply drop your jaw in a relaxed manner; don't push it down. The tip of your tongue is forward and the front of your tongue is raised. Practice singing the words below.

SUN

Topic: IH versus EH

Certain regional dialects tend to substitute *ih* for *eh*. (As someone who grew up in Alabama, I should know!) In such instances, "any" becomes "inny" and "send" becomes "sinned." Remember, for *eh* just drop your jaw a bit more than for *ih*. Keep the jaw comfortably relaxed.

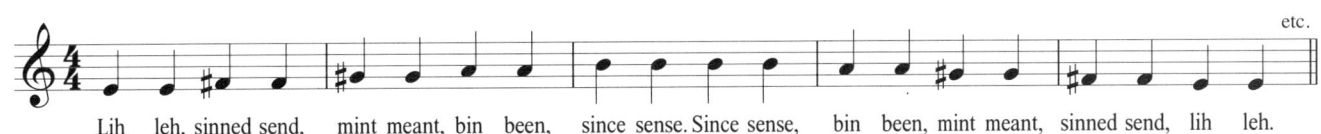

VOCAL AEROBICS — WEEK 3

MON

Topics: Breathing; phonation

This etude may prove to be a challenge at first because we're moving from a voiceless hiss to a voiced hum, moving upward by two steps, then coming back to where we started. Take a good low breath, support the hiss as you exhale, then continue that good support as you move to the hum. Maintain a strong sense of the 4/4 rhythmic pulse, breathing quietly where you see the breath marks. (They look like oversized commas.) Be sure to listen to the demo first.

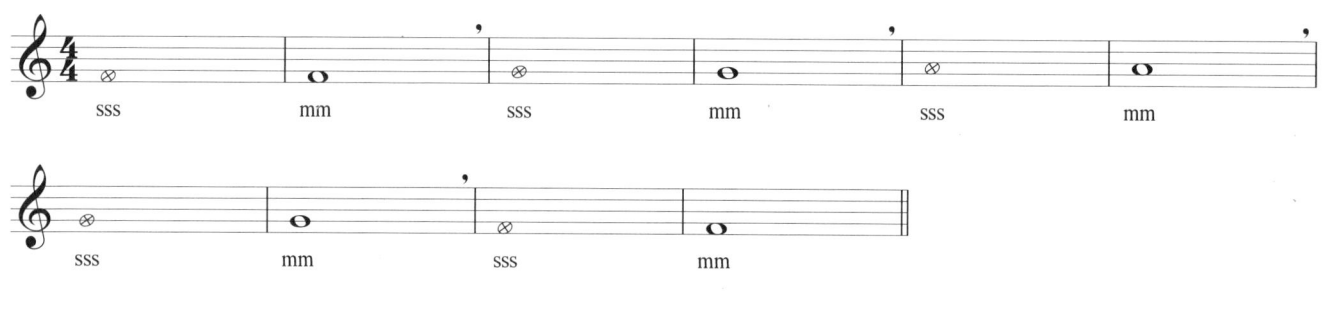

TUE

Topic: EE–IH–EH

Now let's compare the three vowels we've studied. You'll notice that we're moving from closed to open: *ee-ih-eh*.

WED

Topic: Consonants, both voiced/voiceless

We've been singing consonants since the first week of aerobics. Like vowels, they fall into various categories. We will look more closely at this subject in the weeks ahead. Today let's begin by listing two classifications of consonants: *voiced* and *voiceless*. These are easily defined. For a voiced consonant, your vocal cords vibrate; for a voiceless consonant, they don't. Sing the music example below, which uses Fs and Vs. Tomorrow we will discuss these in greater detail.

THU

Topic: Consonants F & V

F is an voiceless consonant; *v* is a voiced consonant. Both are articulated with your lower lip and your upper teeth. For the *f*, you just send the breath through; for the *v*, you need to engage your vocal cords. We can add another descriptor to these two sounds: they are *continuant consonants*. (In other words, their sound can be sustained, unlike, say, *b*, *p*, *t*, or *d*. More on this later.)

FRI

Topic: Consonant, R

A badly sung *r* can really gum up your singing, so follow this simple rule: *Sing an "r" only before a sung vowel sound. Nowhere else!* For example, don't sing the *r* in words like "warm," "heart," "your," and the like. At first, that may feel somewhat affected, but trust me on this. All the words below require an *r* sound, articulated with the tip of your tongue against your gums, just behind your upper front teeth. At all costs, avoid pushing the middle of your tongue to the roof of your mouth. You may find it helpful, at first, to practice by substituting a *d* sound for the *r* sound. Listen to the demo track.

SAT

Topic: Consonant, R (take 2)

As we noted yesterday, an *r* consonant should be sounded only before a sung vowel sound. Using a *d* sound to practice what is called a "rolled *r*" can be helpful. Today's etude provides several examples. Use your best British accent!

SUN

Topic: Consonant, R (take 3)

We want the *r* consonant to be our friend, not our nemesis. Oftentimes, words contain that letter, but it is not sounded *at all* when singing. For example, "warm" becomes "wawm" and "for" becomes "faw." If you think singing that way makes you sound pretentious, please toss that notion out the window right now. All the words in today's aerobic contain unsounded *r* consonants. Have fun!

9

VOCAL AEROBICS
WEEK 4

MON
Topics: Breathing; phonation

Look back at the Monday exercises in Weeks 1 and 3. We're going to expand on those, combining them to make an even more effective warm-up. Practice both of those a few times before you start working on today's aerobic. As before, maintain a strong sense of the 4/4 rhythmic pulse, inhaling quietly where you see the breath marks.

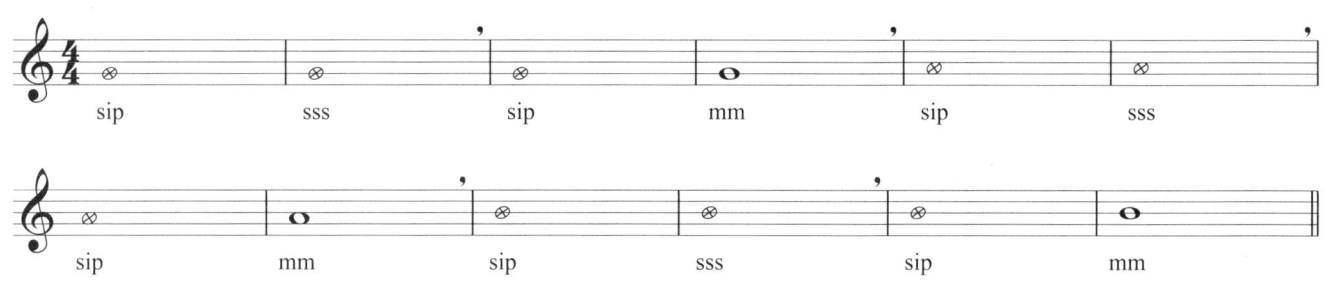

TUE
Topic: AH vowel

Say: "Aha!" You just articulated the most open of all vowels and the lowest of all the back vowels. The tip of your tongue was forward, touching the back of your lower front teeth, and was lying relatively flat in your mouth. Your jaw was dropped, but relaxed. Your soft palate was raised, just like at the doctor's office. And your lips? Well, you shouldn't have been aware of them at all. (In other words, don't protrude your lips for *ah*.) In the exercise below, beware of those treacherous *r* consonants.

WED
Topic: AW vowel

As was the case with *ah*, *aw* is an open back vowel. However, its sound is much darker. The tip of the tongue should be forward, and the back of the tongue is arched. Your lips should be fairly far apart, narrowed at the corners, and pursed far forward, forming an oval shape. (If you watch yourself in a mirror, your mouth will not look absolutely oval, but you should have the feeling that they are shaped that way. Make sense?) Your jaw should be dropped, of course.

THU

Topic: AH versus AW

Too often, vocalists sing *ah* when they should sing *aw*. In the etude below, we alternate these two vowels. The first word uses *ah*, the second uses *aw*. Notice how, for *aw*, your lips must protrude and the back of your tongue must arch a bit.

Mah maw, star war, park lawn, far haul, part bald. Dark taunt, calm morn, palm claw, farm walk, mah maw.

FRI

Topic: OO vowel

Say: "Do you choose blue?" That, obviously, is *oo*, the most closed of all vowels. The tip of the tongue touches the lower front teeth, while the back of the tongue arches toward the soft palate. The lips are rounded and protruded forward to a small opening approximately the size of your little finger. Be careful not to pull your upper lip downward; it should protrude well away from your teeth. Likewise, avoid opening your mouth too much; that will cause the *oo* to sound hooty and swallowed. Use your mirror.

Oo. Too who you. Brute croon prove.
Fruit grew true. Droop plume juice.

SAT

Topic: Alternating AH-OO

Practice the music example below, alternating between *ah* and *oo*. Use only your lips to make this change. Notice how the resonating space of *ah* is needed, even when singing the closed *oo* vowel.

Ah - oo - ah - oo ah - oo - ah - oo - ah. Ah - oo - ah - oo ah - oo - ah - oo - ah.
Ah - oo - ah - oo ah - oo - ah - oo - ah. Ah - oo - ah - oo ah - oo - ah - oo - ah.

SUN

Topic: Vowels, closed to open

As you work through this book, you'll discover that we spend a lot time singing—and talking about—vowel sounds. Why? Because vowels are what carry the sound. It's true that we have consonants that can be sustained, such as the *n* in the example here. And though they can lend incredible opportunities for expression when singing a song, their volume level is nowhere near that of vowels. In this simple exercise, we sing repeated notes, moving from a closed *oo* sound to an open *ah* sound. The *n* allows you to articulate each new note without stopping the sound or your flow of breath.

Noo noh naw nah. Noo noh naw nah. Noo noh naw nah.
Noo noh naw nah. Noo noh naw nah. Noo noh naw nah.

VOCAL AEROBICS

WEEK 5

MON
Topic: Breathing

Here's a good warm-up for those breathing muscles. Expand again on every rest, both quarters and eighths. You should notice that, in the first four bars, air can continue through the *s* and the *f*; we call those continuant consonants. In the last four bars, there's a more explosive quality to the *t* and *k*; we call those stopped consonants. (We will look at consonants more closely later in the book.) All four, however are voiceless consonants. To engage your vocal cords, sing the second set: *z, v, d, g*. First, listen to the online demonstration.

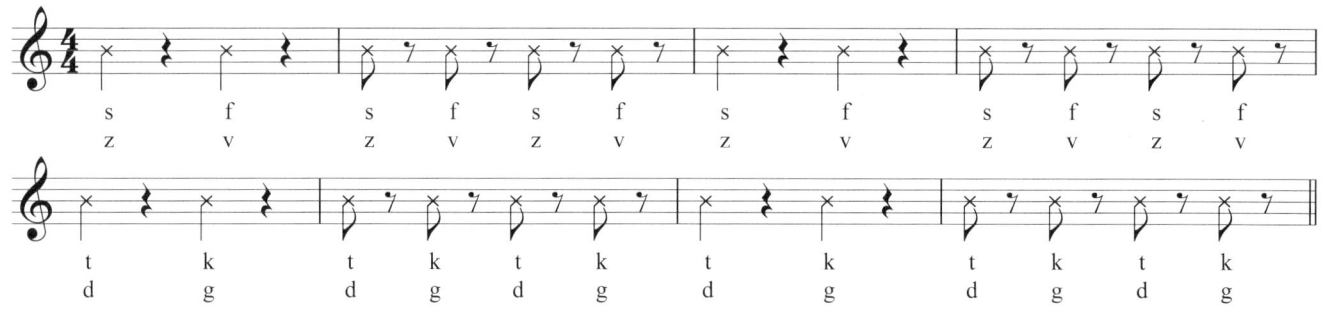

TUE
Topic: EE vowel vs. AH vowel

Say *nee-nah* (much like the name Nina). What do you about the two vowel sounds? That right: One is a closed front vowel (*ee*), the other is an open back vowel (*ah*). They are at opposite ends of the vowel spectrum. Previously, we've used yah (*ee-ah*) to practice moving from one to the other. Here, let's use various rhythm patterns and move quickly and cleanly. The *n* is a pitched continuant consonant that will help you focus the vowel sounds. Listen to the demo first.

WED
Topics: Closed-to-open-to-closed vowels; major triads

Let's use a major-triad arpeggio to move across several vowels: from closed to open, then back to closed. Take notice of how the shape of your mouth changes to form these sounds. Sing both sets, using the initial consonants as shown. Then sing them with only the vowels. Can you describe the physical adjustments you made in moving from one sound to the next?

1. Nee nay neh nay nee.   Nee nay neh nay nee.   Nee nay neh nay nee.   Nee nay neh nay nee.
2. Loo loh lah loh loo.   Loo loh lah loh loo.   Loo loh lah loh loo.   Loo loh lah loh loo.

THU

Topics: Vowel focus

This little exercise is perfect for practicing vowel focus. It will make more sense if you listen to the demo before reading further… Okay. Ready? We're using a voiceless *th* sound (as in "thanks") prior to each vowel. For the five-note scale, sing the first syllable of "Thursday." (We've shown it as *ö*, a German umlaut.) As you move from *ee* to *ay* to *ö*, the vowel becomes more open. The goal is to keep the same forward focus in all three sounds.

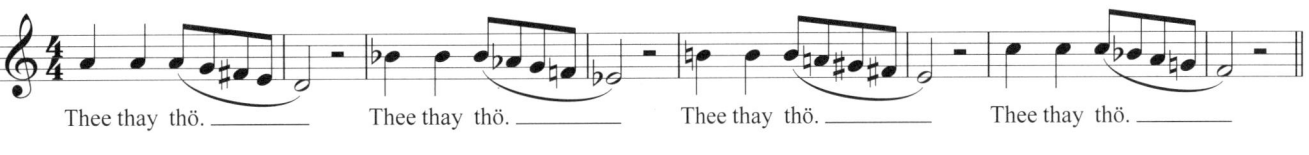

FRI

Topic: Vowels, closed to open

In the music example below, there are two sets of syllables. In each, the vowel sounds move from closed to open. By their very nature, closed vowels are easier to keep centered and in tune than open vowels. As you sing the five repeated notes, strive to retain the same focus across the spectrum. In the top line, the continuant consonant *n* allows you to sing all five sounds without interrupting the sound. Use a voiceless *th* (as in "thanks") on the lower line; the vocal sound is interrupted by the consonant, but your breath flow should never stop. Listen to the demo before you begin.

SAT

Topics: Diphthong information; AH-IH diphthong

A diphthong (DIFF-thong) is a sound comprised of two consecutive vowels in the same syllable. The term is derived from the Greek language: *di-* (meaning two) and *phtongos* (meaning sound). The sound is continuous, with the first vowel sustained and the second vowel added at the very end. Throughout this book, we will look at several diphthongs. Let's begin with *ah-ih*, as in night, eye, I, die, etc. Look at the music example below. This sentence fragment consists only of "And I…" After the quarter-note pickup, sing the *ah* vowel through the series of eighth notes, adding *ih* at the very last second. As always, beware of the half step between mi-fa.

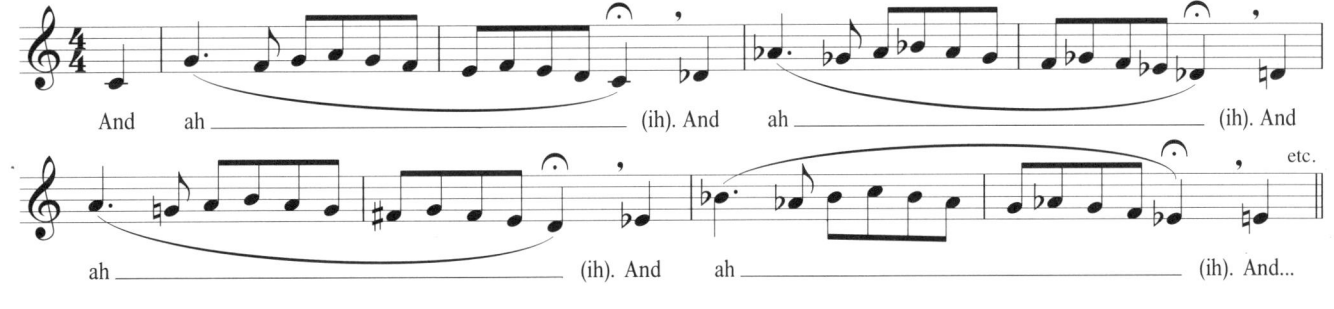

SUN

Topics: Octave scale; intonation; breath management

Octave scales—both ascending and descending—are a common, useful pattern for vocal training. They encourage good support and efficient use of the breath. You'll discover that the breath moves a bit more quickly when ascending, creating a built-in crescendo. The opposite is true when descending: the breath relaxes a bit and the sound has a natural diminuendo. Put your ears to work, being always attentive to singing accurately and in tune. The half-steps between notes three and four (mi-fa) and seven and eight (ti-do) can sometimes be the most treacherous. Sing first on lee, then choose your own vowels.

VOCAL AEROBICS
WEEK 6

MON
Topics: Gently warming up the voice; three-note scale

You've seen this simple melodic pattern before, and will see it again as you continue through the book. Why? Because it is one of the best ways to begin your daily warm-up regimen. We're singing a three-note scale up and then back down, aiming at all times to make sure the top note is well-tuned. Always sing *molto legato* (very smoothly); there should be no "bumps" along the way. Give the dotted-half note a full three beats. The example below has vowel sounds that incrementally move from closed (*ee*) to open (*ah*). Sing it that way, then make up your own series of syllables, covering the full range of your voice. Start mid-range and go higher, moving up a half step for each iteration. When you've reached your highest comfortable note, begin moving down by half steps until you reach your bottom notes.

TUE
Topic: Five-note scale

Throughout *Vocal Aerobics*, we'll use the five-note scale. Today, we'll sing it two ways, first with *mum* on every note, then with a sustained hum. When you hum, your lips are closed, but your jaw is dropped to allow resonance space in your mouth. As you move your breath through the phrases, the volume will naturally increase (*crescendo*) as you ascend and diminish (*diminuendo*) as you come back down. Keep the sound focused—and listen to the online demo before you start.

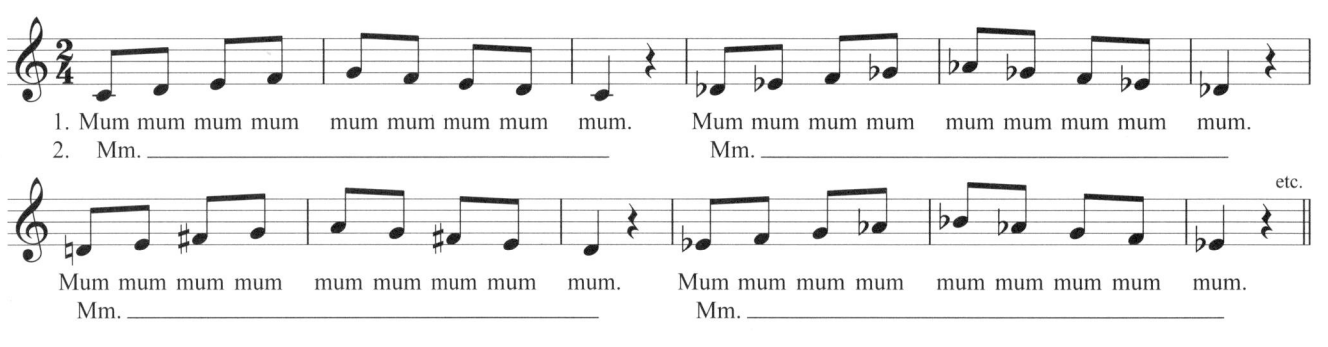

WED
Topics: Flexibility; range

Let's sing an ascending six-note scale and rock back-and-forth on the fifth and sixth notes before coming back down. Eventually, you'll want to sing each three-bar phrase in a single breath on a single vowel sound, as shown below. It might be a good idea, however, to start slowly, breathing as necessary. To make sure your pitches are accurate, articulate a staccato *bim* on each note. Over time, add vowel sounds. This is a good aerobic for vocal agility and for increasing your range.

14

THU

Topic: Warm-up exercise

If you've ever sung in a choir, it's likely that you have encountered an exercise like this. Some choral directors love—pardon the pun—this kind of warm-up. It's a great way to get your lungs and your voice moving, because it covers the range of an octave and calls for beautiful, well-enunciated vowels. The first-person singular pronoun "I" calls for a diphthong—two sounds—*ah* and *ee*. Use a tongue glide for the *ee* and get right back to a big, open *ah* for "lahv." Keep your throat open for the *oo* ("to") and *ee* (sing) vowels. Retain a high, vertical feel throughout.

FRI

Topic: Consonants, L & N

Earlier, we practiced the consonants *f* and *v* (see page 9) and labeled them continuants. Let's add two more: *l* and *n*. Both are voiced consonants, so your vocal cords will vibrate. *L* and *n* are articulated with the tip of your tongue against your gums, just behind your upper front teeth. You will notice that we have used these in quite a few etudes, because they are a great way to get the sound started.

SAT

Topics: Arpeggios, ascending and descending; stepwise motion

Some will remember singing this song in grade school. Who knew that you were practicing arpeggios—both ascending and descending—and stepwise motion? Sing first on the syllables, then on the words. Be expressive, and experiment with different articulations (legato, detached, etc.).

SUN

Topics: Portamento; intervals; intonation; warming up

Sliding from one discrete note to another is called *portamento*. Often employed by trombonists and string players, it's an excellent technique for warming up the voice because it allows us to sing sounds that are between the notes of the piano keyboard. In this aerobic, we use an ascending five-note scale, singing the root and then sliding upward to each note while covering all the microtones in between. Take this one very slowly, inhaling after every measure. No syllables are indicated in the music example, so try several. As suggested previously, start with a hum or the *n* sound we used in Week 1, then try closed vowels like *loo* and *lee*, eventually moving to more open sounds like *loh* and *law*.

VOCAL AEROBICS
WEEK 7

MON

Topics: Phonation; breath management; dynamics

For this etude, choose a slow but comfortable tempo. Across a five-note scale, ascending then descending, start each note *piano* (soft) and *crescendo* (increase the volume) to *forte* (loud). We effect a crescendo by speeding up our breath as we hold the note. Incite each pitch gently, allowing the initial *l* to help you focus the sound. The music example below uses *oo*, a closed, back vowel; sing other syllables as well, such as *lee, lay, ley, loh,* and *lah*. Listen to the singer on the demo track before you start.

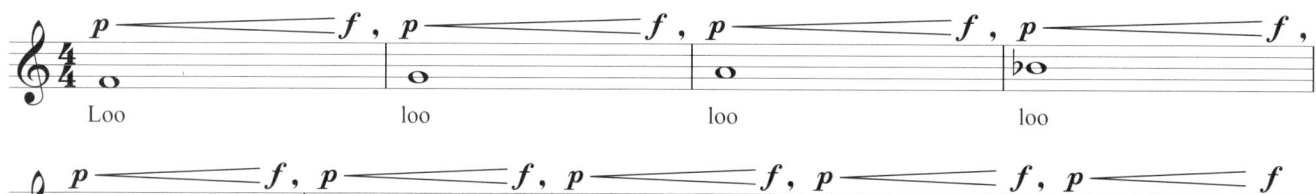

TUE

Topic: Two-note phrases, ascending/descending

The two-note phrase is a melodic figure often encountered in music of many styles. It can be quite expressive when approached with the requisite sensitivity and musicality. The first note receives more emphasis than the first; there is a sigh-like quality to it. The two-note gesture can be the same two notes or any interval. Here, we'll practice singing in thirds, outlining a major triad.

WED

Topics: Lip trill; breath management; warm-up

Say "brrrr" like you're cold. Did you feel your lips vibrate? We call that a lip trill (or lip roll). It is an excellent diagnostic tool, one that ensures a tension-free throat, because it's impossible to sing a lip trill and tighten your neck muscles at the same time. You may find it easier to articulate a lip trill if you place your two index fingers on either side of your mouth; then just send the air through your lips. You can do that without making a vocal sound, of course, but here we're going to use a simple three-note phrase. Listen to the demo track.

THU

Topic: Portamento, up/down a fifth

As a kid, did you ever have a slide whistle? Those were fun! Trombones operate on the same principle. We going to imitate their ability to slide up and down, using a *portamento*. For now, we'll slide up the interval of a fifth and come back down again. Take a good low breath and sing a well-focused hum. Move slowly and feel the surge of air as you ascend; keep the sound supported as you descend. Move up by half steps. Listen to the demo before you begin.

FRI

Topics: Warming up; getting the breath moving

Here's a fun, if somewhat silly-sounding, exercise. The *b* consonant will get your lips working, the *d* consonant will get your tongue moving, the *ee* vowel will get the sound focused, and the alternating vowels in the second phrase will change the resonance space inside your mouth. On top of all that, your breath stream takes the phrase upward and then back down. Wow! Simple, but so useful!

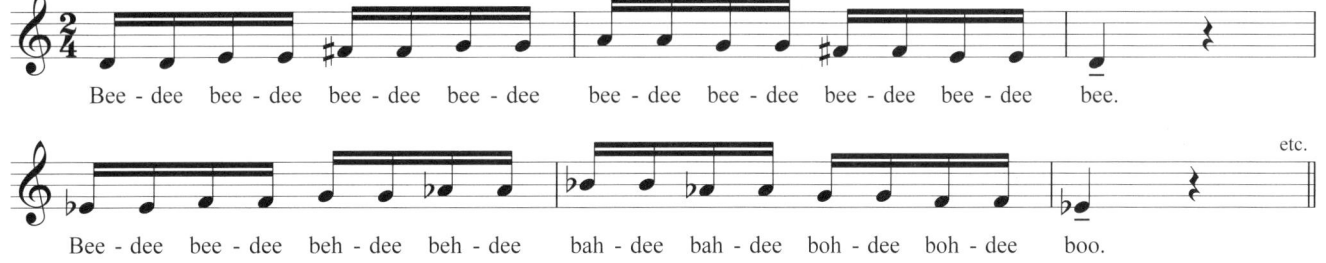

SAT

Topic: Summary of intervals

Let's review the intervals found in a major scale, using the root note (tonic) as our home base. Take a look at the music example below. First, we sing a second, then a third, and so forth—until we reach the octave; then we sing what is essentially a mirror image. At first, go as slowly as you need to, breathing as needed. The ultimate goal, however, is to sing each four-bar phrase in a single breath. Practice staccato (*ting*) and legato (*ah*). Use the piano to verify your pitch accuracy.

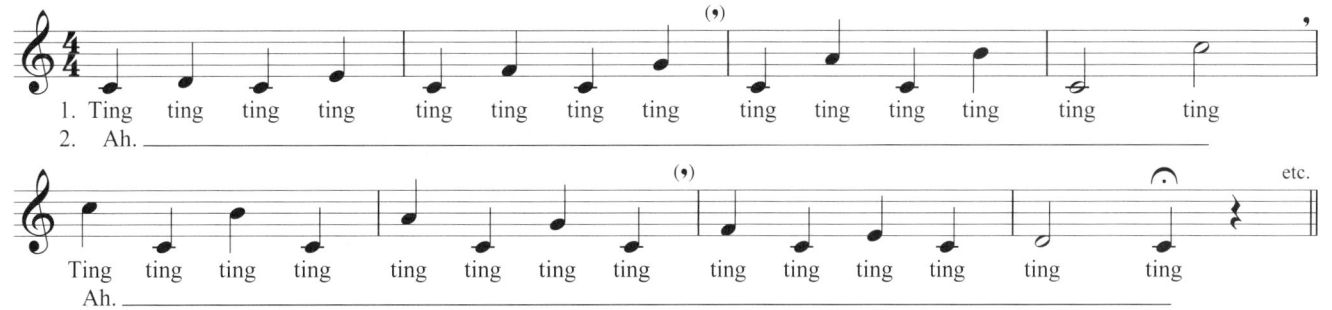

SUN

Topic: Legato; warming up

Let's expand the five-note scale by a step and sing a six-note scale. This is a good warm-up for everyday use. Sing *molto legato* (very smoothly) and keep the vowel centered. You'll feel a natural crescendo as you ascend; work to keep the sound full as you descend. The music example shows *mee*, but use other vowels of your own choosing.

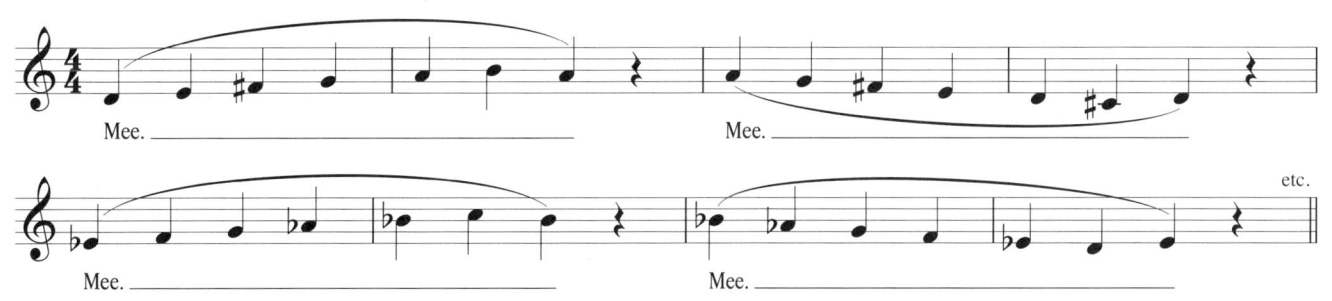

WEEK 8

One of the unique features of *Vocal Aerobics* is the opportunity to put to practical use the singing ability you have acquired. To that end, we'll learn a song every eight weeks. Folksongs, hymns, carols, and The Great American Songbook will be included.

Song preparation requires any number of skills and decisions. Obviously, in this book we're choosing the songs for you, based on their appropriate level of difficulty and the concepts that need to be reinforced. But when selecting a song on your own, consider the following:

- Do you prefer a short song or a long one?
- An easy song or one that is more challenging?
- Do the words have special meaning?
- How do you react to the melody and backing harmonies?
- Do you prefer a slow ballad or an up-tempo number?
- What musical style most appeals to you? Pop? Folk? Classical? Rock?

Our first selection is a folksong from Wales, "All Through the Night." As with any song, its text, its tempo, its musical form, its overall mood, and its vocal range need to be taken into account. All these aspects will affect the learned concepts and singing techniques we need to draw upon. With that in mind, let's take a closer look.

There are 16 measures. Notice that m. 1-4 = m. 5-8 = m. 13-16. Bars 9-12 are different. (In common parlance, we call those four measures the "bridge.") Just by a quick analysis of the form, we can see already that, in terms of notes and rhythms, we have only eight measures to learn.

The tempo marking says "Moderately, gently." Reading the words, we discover that this is a lullaby, so we know from the outset that we're not going to be singing in a loud, up-tempo style. Take a look at the punctuation of the text; observe the shape of the vocal line. What do you extrapolate from that information? That's correct: Generally, we're going to sing in two- and four-bar increments.

Okay, so now how shall we go about practicing? If the song is unfamiliar, you might want to bend an ear to the demo track. As you listen, use an erasable pencil—never mark your music in ink!—and add the breath-mark apostrophes in the spots you think you might want to inhale. Now use the piano-only track and hum the melody, breathing at the places you've marked.

This is important: It's best not to start with the words. Rather, as stated above, begin with a well-focused hum. After that, sing the melody on closed vowels such as *oo* and *ee*. When you're proficient with those, move onto more open sounds like *eh* and *ah*. As you practice in this manner, experiment with phrase shape and dynamics (see below). When you're ready to sing the words, your approach should be simple and sincere. As you can see, there's nothing dramatic here!

If you took piano lessons or played in orchestra or band, this information will be familiar and you can skip it. If, however, music reading is not your strong suit, take a few minutes to look it over.

pp = pianissimo (very soft)
p = piano (soft)
mp = mezzo piano (moderately soft)
mf = mezzo forte (moderately loud)
f = forte (loud)
ff = fortissimo (very loud)

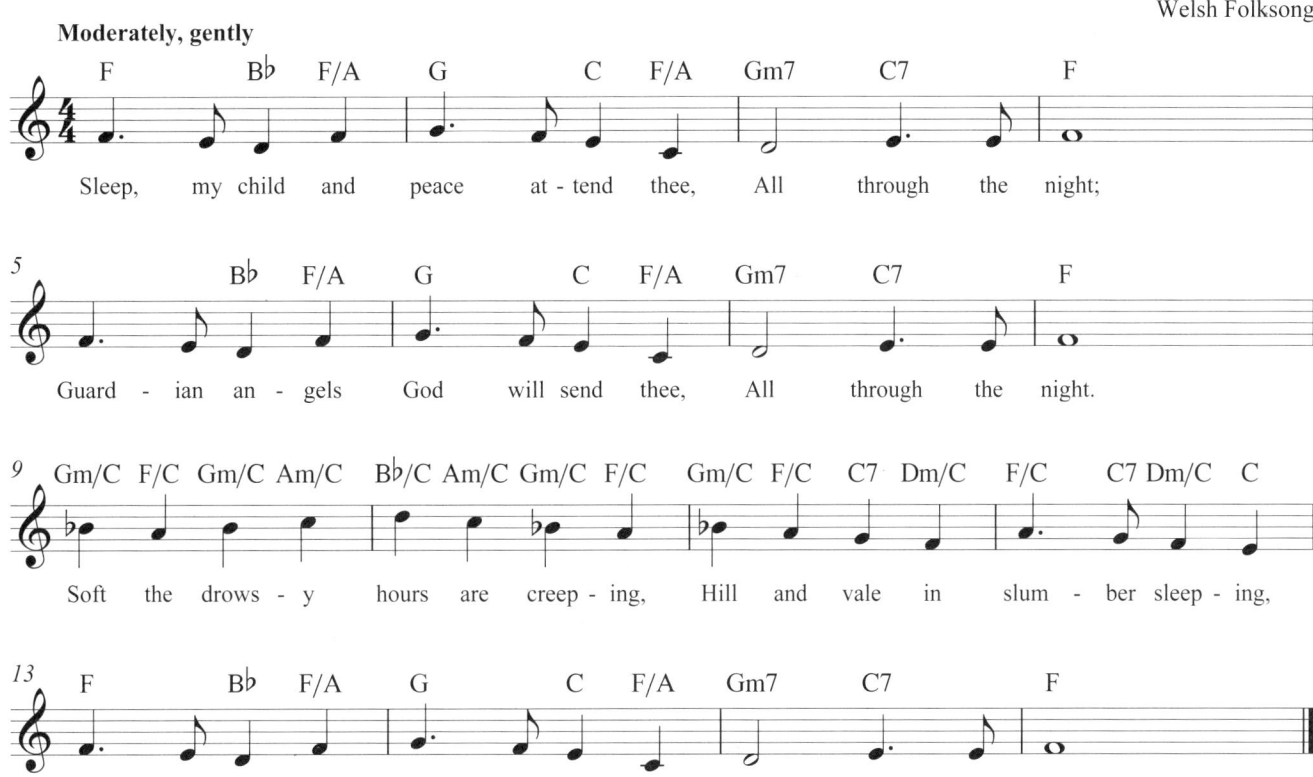

VOCAL AEROBICS — WEEK 9

MON

Topics: Phonation; breath management; dynamics

Let's continue with the concept we practiced in Week 7, but sing it in reverse, moving from forte to piano. We call getting gradually softer a *diminuendo*. It is often a bit more challenging than the *crescendo*, because we're regulating a change from a loud sound with fast-moving air to a soft sound with slow-moving air. The music example below uses *ee*, a closed, front vowel; as before, sing other syllables as well, such as *loo*, *loh*, *law*, and *lah*.

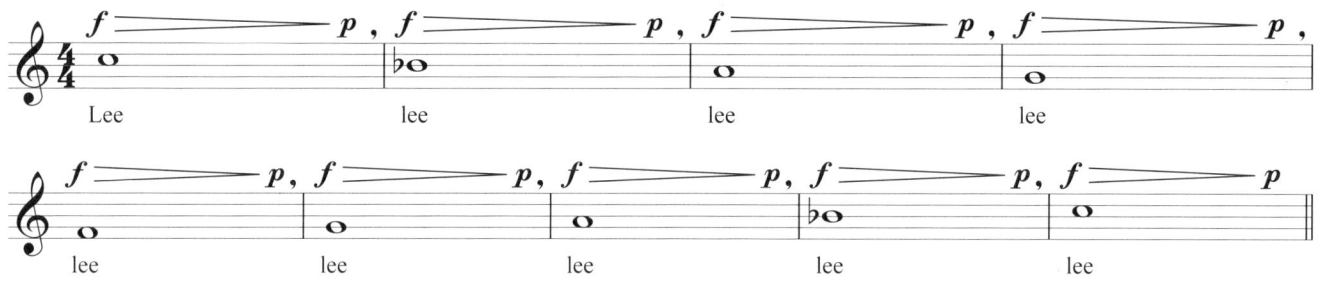

TUE

Topic: Descending major scale using two-note phrases

As you'll see throughout *Vocal Aerobics*, the major scale offers all sorts of possibilities for warm-ups. In this case, we sing down the scale, employing two-note phrases. As noted earlier, it's customary, when singing or playing that simple melodic figure, to lean into the first pitch and slightly relax the sound on the second one. (Listen to the audio track for a demonstration.) We accomplish this by speeding up the breath on pitch 1 and letting it slow a bit on pitch 2. At first, breathe as often as you need to. The goal, though, is to sing each four-bar phrase in a single breath.

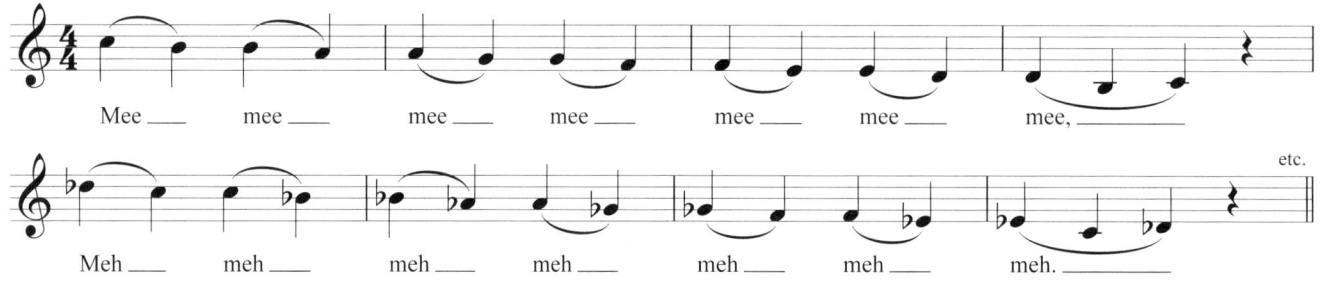

WED

Topic: Gently warming up the voice

Let's take an exercise from Monday of Week 6 a step further. Review that one first. Now, before singing the three-note scale, we are going to add a measure with a gentle eighth-note pulse on each beat. Make sure each of those first four notes is well-supported and that you're employing a balanced onset for each. If need be, catch a breath before measure 2 of each pattern. Use the vowels shown, then choose your own. Cover your comfortable range.

THU

Topics: Portamento; intervals; intonation; warming up

Today's exercise reverses the one we learned in Week 6. Here, we're using a descending fifth, then fourth, and so on, starting with the top note and sliding down to the root note. Sing slowly, observing the breath marks. Cover as many microtones as you can. Start with a hum, then use several different vowels of your choosing.

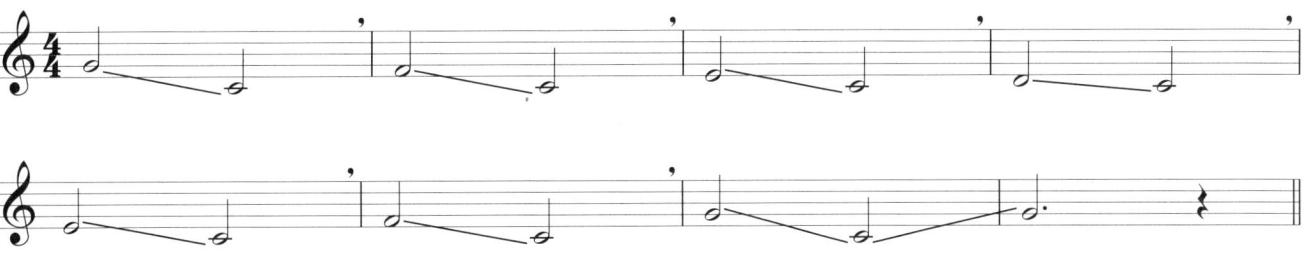

FRI

Topics: Warming up; singing legato; vowel uniformity

This warm-up is a favorite of singers, voice teachers, and choir directors. Why? Because it is so simple, yet so effective. We sing a five-note major scale from top to bottom then back up again. Singing molto legato, the goal is to maintain a well-shaped vowel. Because we're starting at the top, we're always assured that we won't strain for any notes or tighten our throats. "Ride" the breath evenly, and give the final dotted-half note its full value. Start with the vowels given below, then mix it up as you like.

SAT

Topic: Falsetto for men

As noted in the Introduction, voice teachers often speak of the vocal registers: head voice and chest voice. Women more naturally sing in head voice, while men sing in chest voice. Nevertheless, every voice possesses both, though one may naturally be more developed than the other. This exercise is designed for male voices, though female voices can use it as well. We're singing—at the notated pitch—a descending broken chord across an octave, moving down by half steps. Aim for a light, hooty, owl-like sound. You'll discover that you need faster air to start. Regulate the air flow as you descend, and try to keep only the head voice engaged. Listen to the online demo before you begin.

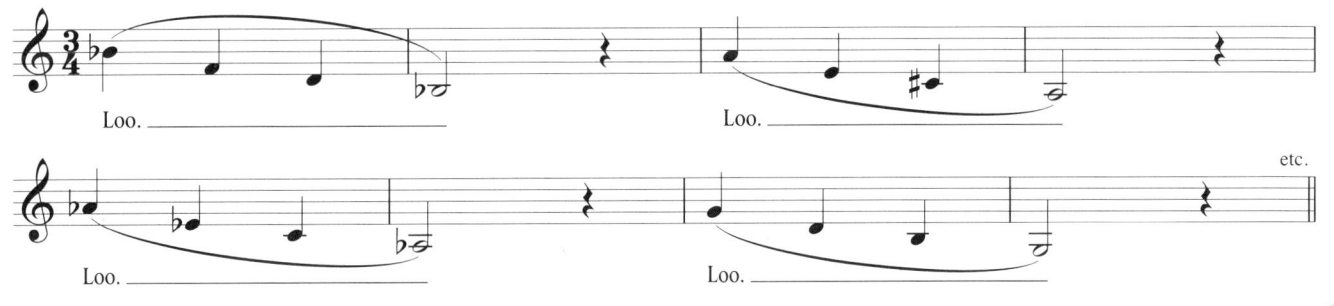

SUN

Topic: Consonants, B & P

We use our lips to articulate the consonants *b* and *p*. When singing lip consonants, make sure your lips remain relaxed; don't press them together. That way, you'll tend to keep your throat relaxed as well. Notice that *b* and *p* are similarly executed, but *b* is voiced and *p* is voiceless.

VOCAL AEROBICS — WEEK 10

MON
Topics: Breath support; flexibility; vowels; warm-up

Here's an etude that's useful on several fronts: breath management, flexibility, articulation, and vowels. It is an excellent tool for warming up. Give a good abdominal "push" to the staccato notes and ensure that they are clean and well-supported. Use a steady stream of breath to ride across the legato 16th notes. Give full value to the concluding quarter note.

TUE
Topic: Preliminary study for EH-IH diphthong

Today's etude is a preliminary exercise for tomorrow's new diphthong. Sing "ah-wet" slowly, placing a well-articulated *t* on each rest. Note that we start with a repeated note, then move up the major five-note scale and back down again. Breathe on the rests (after the Ts) and keep the sound strong. Listen to the demo track.

WED
Topic: EH-IH diphthong

Building on yesterday's aerobic, we add the secondary vowel sound *ih* to form the *eh-ih* diphthong. The word is "await." Hold the *eh* sound until the last second, then sing the *ih* and the final consonant. As you sustain the dotted-half note, keep both the vowel sound and your tone steady. Use good support. We have notated only the ascending five-note pattern. If you like, sing the descending scale as well.

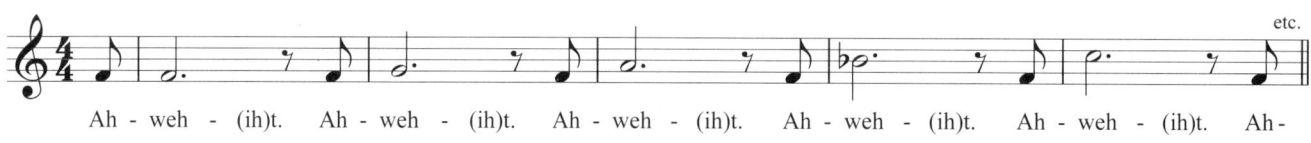

THU

Topics: Major third vs. minor third; bluesy feel

Let's continue practicing half steps. Sing an ascending five-note major scale. As you descend, add an extra note: the minor third. Listen to the demo track. Do you notice how the added pitch and the triplet rhythm lend a bluesy feel? Sing the syllables as shown below, then, just for fun, make up your own lyrics—corny, sentimental, or otherwise!

1. Doo doo doo doo   doo doo doo ____ doo.   Doo doo doo doo   doo doo doo ____ doo.
2. Dee. ____   Dee. ____

Doo doo doo doo   doo doo doo ____ doo.   Doo doo doo doo   doo doo doo ____ doo.   etc.
Dee. ____   Dee. ____

FRI

Topics: Five-note major scale; M consonant

Today we'll use the five-note major scale to get our breath and vocal cords moving. The silly lyrics here make good use of the continuant *m* sound. In this instance, shortchange the vowels and get to the *m* as quickly as possible. It's a great way to focus the sound. Have fun!

Mom-my made me   mash my   M   &   Ms.   Mom-my made me   mash my   M   &   Ms.

Mom-my made me   mash my   M   &   Ms.   Mom-my made me   mash my   M   &   Ms.   etc.

SAT

Topics: Six-note scale; warm-up

Ride your breath as you ascend the six-note major scale, giving a little extra crescendo on the quarter-note at the top. Keep the sound smoothly connected throughout, and sing this etude across your comfortable range. It's a great warm-up tool. Use the syllables given below, then choose others.

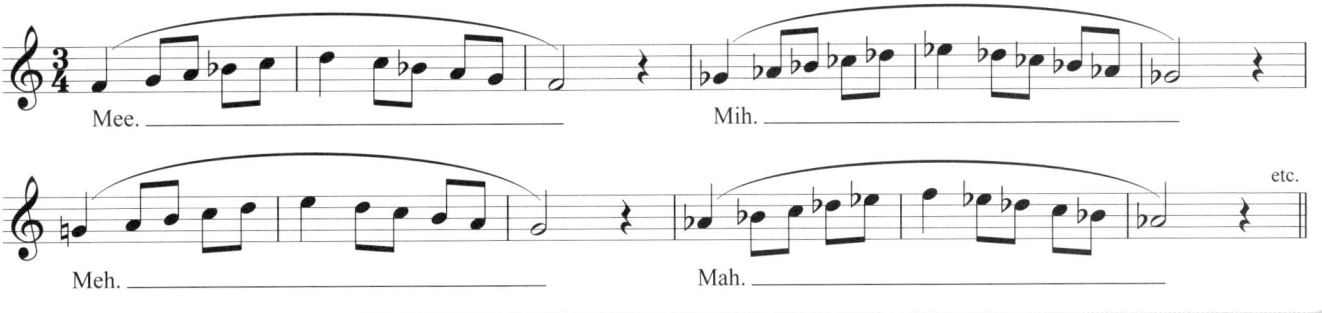

Mee. ____   Mih. ____

Meh. ____   Mah. ____   etc.

SUN

Topic: Singing expressively

Today, let's sing a real melody! Here are the first two (identical) phrases of an old Irish melody, usually sung to the words "Down by the Salley Gardens." The goal here is to give shape and expressivity to the phrases, even though we're not singing the actual words. The goal note, so to speak, is the half note in bar 2; crescendo toward it, then allow the second half of the phase to taper off. Eventually, you'll want to sing the four-bar phrase in a single breath; you may want to use the optional breaths to start. Practice two ways: 1) sing *loo* on every note; 2) sing each phrase on a single *loo*. Choose other vowels as well. The demo track is a good model to follow.

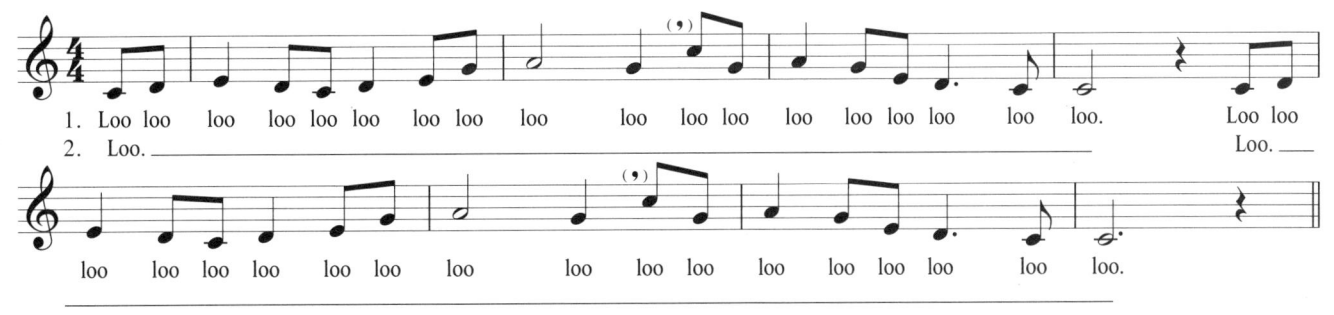

1. Loo loo   loo   loo loo loo   loo loo   loo   loo   loo loo   loo   loo loo loo   loo   loo.   Loo loo
2. Loo. ____   Loo. ____

loo   loo loo loo   loo loo   loo   loo   loo loo   loo   loo loo loo   loo   loo.

23

VOCAL AEROBICS — WEEK 11

MON

Topics: Phonation; breath management; dynamics; *messa di voce*

This challenging exercise combines two earlier ones from Weeks 7 and 9. We begin piano, crescendo to forte, then diminuendo back to piano—all in one breath! It's what the Italian voice teachers of earlier centuries called *messa di voce* ("placing of voice"). The diminuendo definitely is the harder task. Make sure you stay connected to your breathing muscles; never allow the muscles of your neck/throat to engage. No syllables are indicated in the music example, so try several. Start with a hum or the *n* sound we used in Week 1, then try closed vowels like *loo* and *lee*, eventually moving to more open sounds like *loh* and *law*.

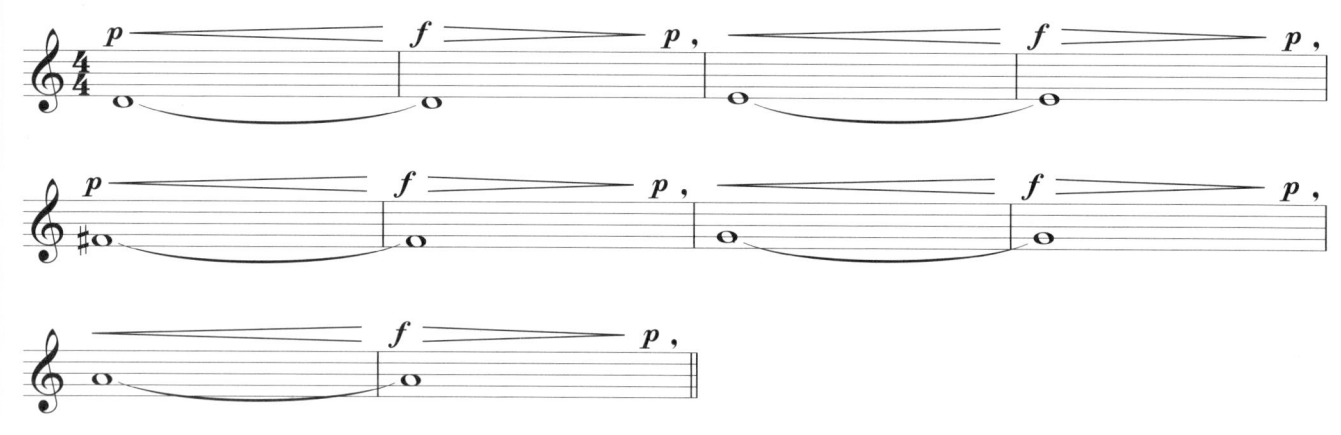

TUE

Topics: Minor key; legato; phrase shape; text enunciation; 3/4 time

Look at the music example below. Yes, it's just a simple five-note minor scale, but oh the potential it holds! The etude is set in 3/4 time, with a long-short rhythm in every bar. Sing first on the syllables, molto legato, and with an expressive shape to the phrase. When you're ready to add the text, really ham it up and go for melodrama. But before singing the words, speak them like a Shakespearean actor projecting to the back row of a large theatre. Capitalize on the expressive potential of the consonants; use the vowels to keep the sound connected. Listen to the demo.

WED

Topics: Breath; articulation; note lengths; legato

This ingenious little four-bar etude allows you to practice several varieties of articulation: detached, staccato, tenuto, and legato. The first measure is simply detached, the second employs staccato and eighth-note tenutos, the third calls for quarter-note tenutos, and the fourth is a five-note scale sung legato. In each case, commence with a balanced onset. (See page 2.) We've suggested a couple of syllables to get you started. Make up your own thereafter.

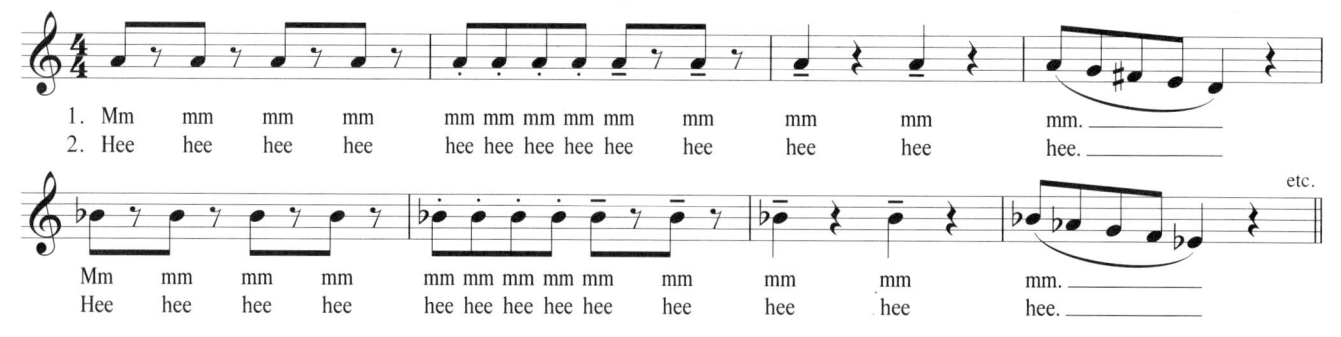

THU

Topics: Chest voice; AH vowel

Today we expand on an exercise from Week 1. Review that one, then follow it with this new one. On the last three notes of each iteration, there's an upward leap of a fifth. The goal is to keep the well-focused *ah* sound as you jump back to the starting note. Practice this leap two ways: 1) move cleanly from the bottom note to the top and back again; 2) use a glissando, covering the microtones in between the root and fifth. Practice this etude across your entire voice range. The demo is a good model to imitate.

Yah yah yah yah yah. _____ Yah yah yah yah yah. _____ Yah yah yah yah yah. _____

FRI

Topics: Range extension; breath management; vowel focus

This simple octave leap is an effective tool for working on range extension, breath management, and vowel focus. The bottom note of each iteration requires support, of course; but you'll soon realize that the breath doesn't need to move as fast as it does for the top note. Think of it as "fat air" and the top note as "fast air." The *ay* vowel will help you find the center of the *ah* vowel. Crescendo through the dotted-half note. Continue moving up by half steps until you reach your highest comfortable note, then stop. Avoid any tension in your throat; let your breathing muscles do the heavy lifting.

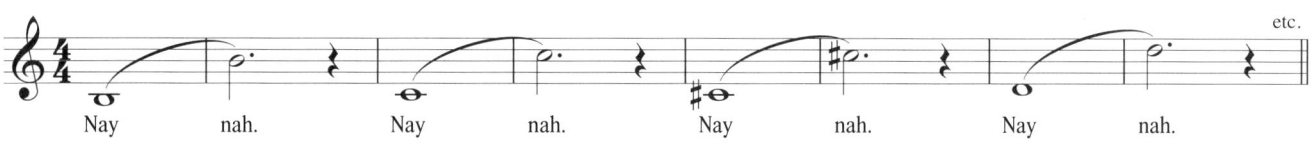

Nay nah. Nay nah. Nay nah. Nay nah. Nay nah.

SAT

Topic: AW-IH diphthong

The two sounds of the *aw-ih* diphthong are *aw* (as in "law") and *ih* (as in "lit"). To sing *aw*, your lips should protrude a bit and have an oval shape; otherwise, you'll get an *ah* vowel. Our practice word is "joy." Keep the rounded sound until the last second, when you add *ih*. Breathe as you need to, but your final goal is a five-bar phrase, as shown in the music example.

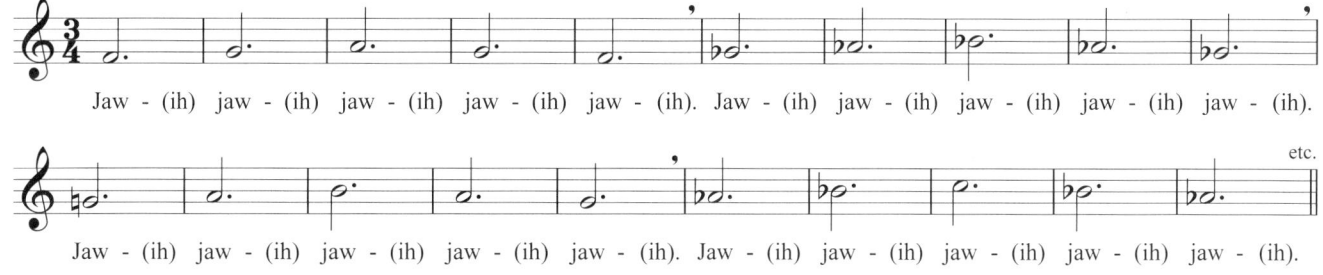

Jaw-(ih) jaw-(ih) jaw-(ih) jaw-(ih) jaw-(ih). Jaw-(ih) jaw-(ih) jaw-(ih) jaw-(ih) jaw-(ih).

Jaw-(ih) jaw-(ih) jaw-(ih) jaw-(ih) jaw-(ih). Jaw-(ih) jaw-(ih) jaw-(ih) jaw-(ih) jaw-(ih).

SUN

Topic: Natural minor scale

There's something different about this melody that is different from the ones we've sung thus far. Just by looking, can you tell what it is? That's correct! It is in a minor key, and contains all the notes of the D natural minor scale. It is based on an old Hebrew song called "Hatikvah." The music example suggests some syllables and places to breathe, but feel free to use your own choices.

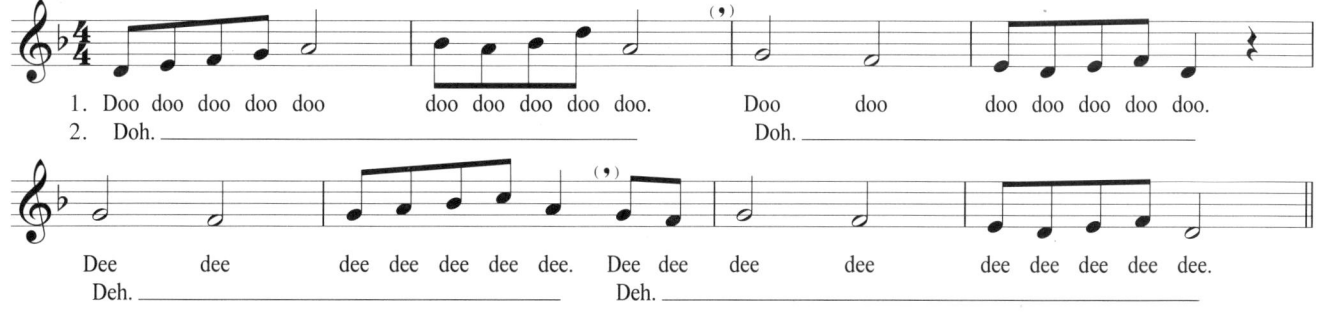

1. Doo doo doo doo doo   doo doo doo doo doo.   Doo doo   doo doo doo doo doo.
2. Doh. _____   Doh. _____

Dee dee   dee dee dee dee dee.   Dee dee dee dee   dee dee dee dee dee.
Deh. _____   Deh. _____

VOCAL AEROBICS — WEEK 12

MON

Topics: Moving from closed to open vowels; spacious AH

Nearly every singer finds *ah* to be one of the most challenging vowels, because there are so many variables that can go awry. Use this simple exercise, sliding down a fifth, to reinforce your good singing of it. As you descend, covering the microtones between the two notes, note what happens inside your mouth. Feel your throat open, your soft palate rise, and the back of your tongue lower. Doesn't that feel nice?

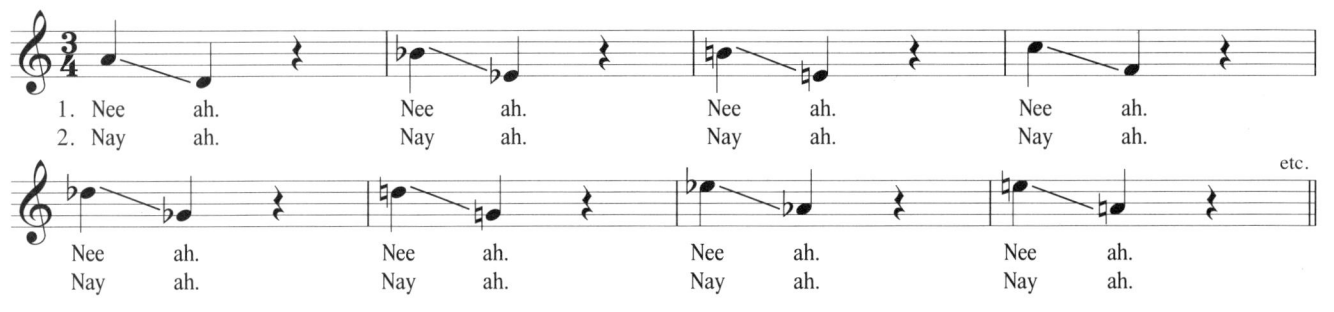

TUE

Topic: Consonants, the two TH sounds

Say: "These, those, they." Now say: "Thin, think, Thursday." What do you notice? Yes, though all the words begin with *th*, the first set used a voiced sound, while the second set was voiceless. For all *th* sounds, place the tip of your tongue lightly against the edge of your upper front teeth. When a voiced sound is needed, engage your vocal cords; when a voiceless sound is called for, send your breath over your tongue.

WED

Topic: Falsetto for men

In Week 9, we talked about the vocal registers and male falsetto. This aerobic uses a three-note scale, descending then ascending. To begin, find a comfortable note in your head voice, using the aspirant *h* and the closed *oo* vowel. (You want to sound like an owl.) Sing the melodic pattern as notated below, breathe (as indicated), move down a half step and repeat. Continue this process until you discover that your chest voice wants to take over. Be sure to listen to the demo track.

THU

Topic: Two-note phrases, descending/ascending
In Week 7, we practiced two-note phrases outlining a triad. Let's do that again today. This time, we'll descend and then go back up again. Remember to stress the first note and allow the second note to be a bit quieter.

Leh — lay — lee — lay — leh.   Lah — loh — loo — loh — lah.

FRI

Topics: Staccato; phonation; breath management
Let's aim for several things here, including efficient breathing, clean staccato attack, good intonation, and focused vowel sounds. We're singing major triads as arpeggios (broken chords), using both quarter notes and eighth notes, moving up a half-step for each iteration. Take a good, low breath before each two-bar phrase. Leave a little daylight, as it were, after each staccato note, but give full rhythmic value to the final note of each phrase. The two vowels in the music example below are at opposite ends of the spectrum: *ee* is a closed, front vowel; *ah* is an open, back vowel. Feel free to add others that fall somewhere in between, such as *heh*, *hoh*, and *haw*.

1. Hee hee hee hee   hee hee hee hee hee.   Hee hee hee hee   hee hee hee hee hee.
2. Hah hah hah hah   hah hah hah hah hah.   Hah hah hah hah   hah hah hah hah hah.

Hee hee hee hee   hee hee hee hee hee.   Hee hee hee hee   hee hee hee hee hee.
Hah hah hah hah   hah hah hah hah hah.   Hah hah hah hah   hah hah hah hah hah.

SAT

Topics: Warm-up; singing legato; vowel uniformity
This vocalise, like Friday's in Week 9, is a favorite. Here, we sing a five-note major scale from bottom to top then back down again. Sing smoothly and crescendo as you ascend; a natural diminuendo will occur on the way down. Use this throughout your comfortable range, making sure you stop when it gets too high; don't strain for any notes or tighten your throat. Use vowels of your choosing, but start with those given below.

1. Noo. _____   Noh. _____
2. Nee. _____   Nay. _____

Naw. _____   Nah. _____
Neh. _____   Nah. _____

SUN

Topic: Register transition, chest to head
Here's another aerobic for moving from chest voice to head voice. Begin lightly—but not breathy—in chest voice, allowing head voice mix in as you go higher. The *g* consonant will help launch you into each phrase. Use a push of breath to sing up and over the three-note scale.

Goo. _____   Goo. _____   Goo. _____   Goo. _____

Goo. _____   Goo. _____   Goo. _____   Goo. _____

VOCAL AEROBICS
WEEK 13

MON
Topic: Consonants, D & T

D and *t* are both tip-of-the-tongue consonants. We can use an additional term to label them: *stop-plosive*. This means the air is stopped—in this case, by the tongue—then released to create the sound. Place the tip of your tongue against your gums, just behind your upper front teeth. As you quickly drop your tongue, emit a puff of air for *t* and a vocal sound for *d*. (*D* is voiced; *t* is voiceless.)

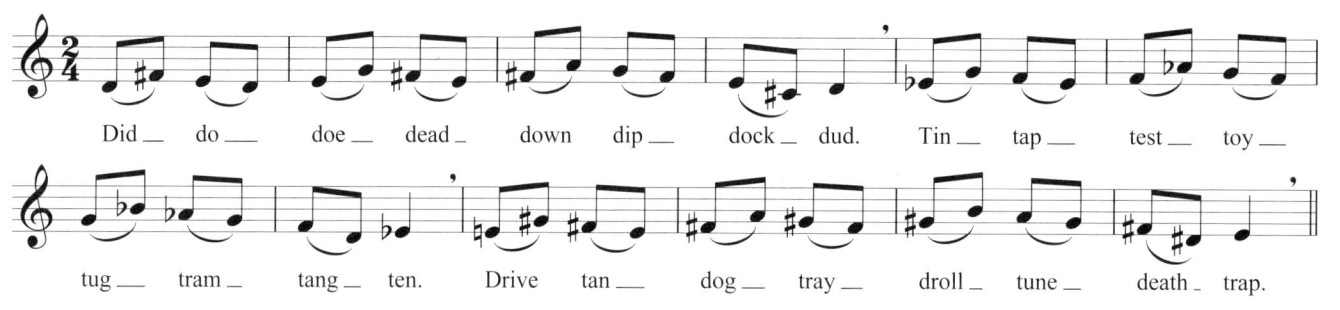

TUE
Topics: Staccato; phonation; breath management

In Week 12 we encountered this vocalise, but starting on the root of the chord, rather than its top note. Once again, let's strive for efficient breathing, clean staccato attack, good intonation, and focused vowel sounds. Sing two-bar phrases, allowing a bit of space each staccato note, but giving full rhythmic value to the final note of each phrase. Sing *haw* and *heh*, as shown in the music example—then employ other vowels of your choosing.

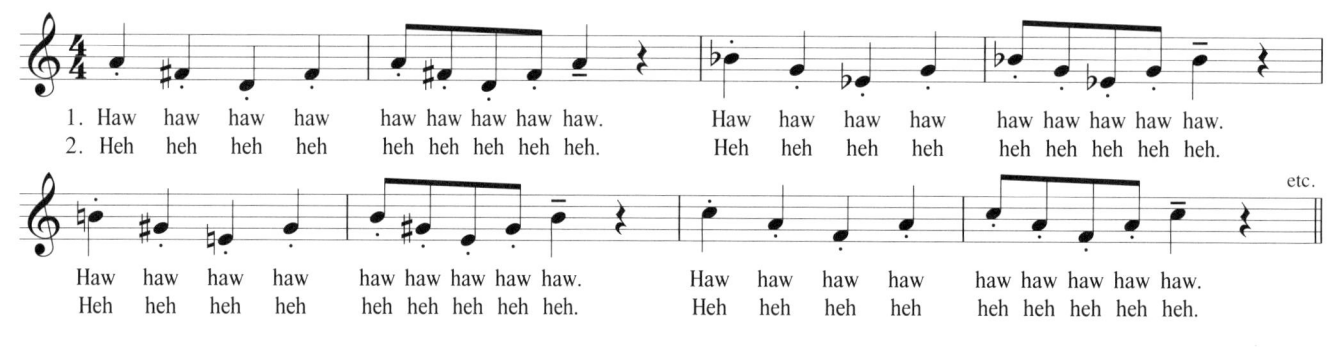

WED
Topic: AH-OO diphthong

Speak: "How now, brown cow?" What vowels were required to articulate that question? Yes, *ah* and *oo*, the two sounds that comprise the *ah-oo* diphthong. In the music example below, we've spelled it out for you in the first two measures. It's up to you to put it into practice with the triad arpeggio in bars 3 and 4. Sustain the *ah*, adding the *oo* at the very end. Other words that utilize this diphthong include plow, thou, shout, ground, and proud.

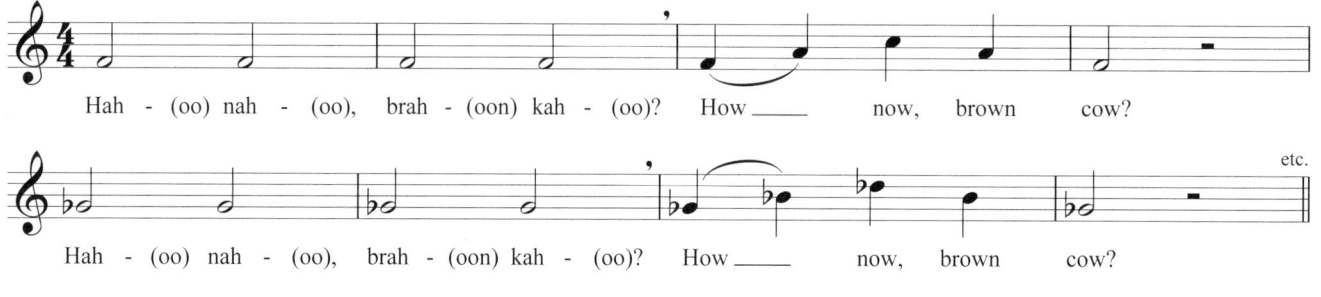

THU

Topics: Major scale descending; 3/4 time

How many ways can we practice a major scale? Innumerable, seemingly. Today, we're singing in a waltz-like 3/4 time, descending with a long-short rhythm in each bar. Be careful of the half-step between the leading tone and the tonic, both on the top and the bottom of the scale. Use the indicated syllables, legato, then add the second line of text. Feel free to make up your own cheesy words as well.

FRI

Topics: Compound meter; pitch accuracy

This melody may sound familiar, and for good reason. It is an excerpt from F.A. Particela's "Mexican Hat Dance." Notice several things: 1) it is in G major, courtesy of the key signature, F#; 2) it is in 6/8 time, a *compound meter*, which means the dotted-quarter note gets the beat, not the quarter note; 3) there are several accidentals, requiring you to sing accurate half steps. Take it slowly at first, always singing a bright *ah* vowel. Increase the tempo as you become more familiar with the tune. Have fun with it!

SAT

Topics: Vocal focus; vowel focus

N and *ng* are great consonants for focusing the voice and the vowels. Both are continuants that bring the vocal sound to a focal point. Let's use them today, in collaboration with *ay*. Sing up a five-note major scale and back down again. This is a useful warm-up, so employ it across your entire range.

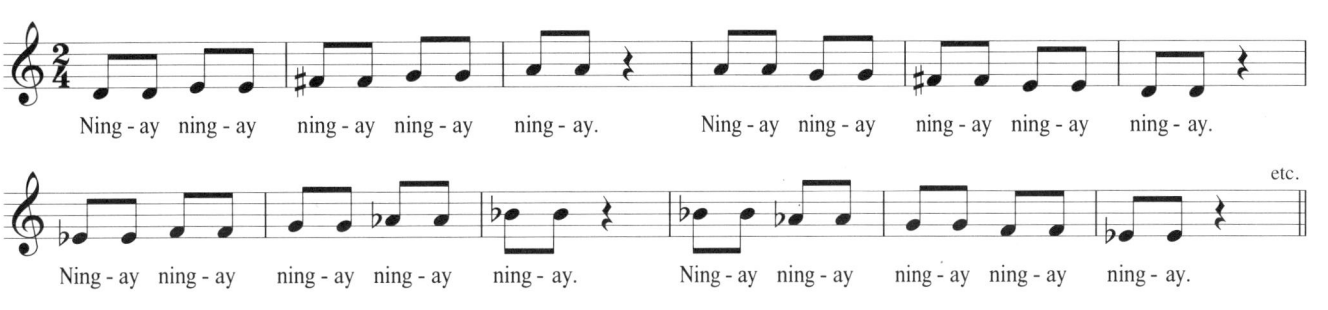

SUN

Topics: Two-note phrases; five-note scale

Let's mix it up by combining descending two-note phrases with the ascending five-note scale. When you begin, feel free to catch a breath where you need it; ultimately, though, you'll want to be able to sing two measures in a single inhalation. Crescendo as you sing up the scale in bar 2, using fast air.

VOCAL AEROBICS
WEEK 14

MON
Topics: Major triad arpeggios, ascending/descending; compound meter
One of the first things you'll notice is the 6/8 time signature. We're singing major-chord arpeggios across an octave, moving up a half step for each repetition. As you ascend, feel a surge of breath (fast air) and crescendo up and over; adjust the breath pressure as you descend. We've indicated several sounds, but choose your own as well.

TUE
Topic: Balanced onset
Remember the three varieties of onset? (See page 2.) This aerobic—a triad arpeggio—allows you to experience a balanced onset. Practice two ways: 1) inhale on each rest, pumping the abdominal muscles; 2) sing three bars in a single breath, inhaling on the quarter rests. If the initial *h* causes you to lose too much air and to sound breathy, omit it. Just sing *oh-oh-oh*.

WED
Topics: Vowel focus; strengthening the voice
Here's a great way to improve vowel focus and to strengthen your voice at the same time. Take a look at the music example below. You'll see that there are several components, in terms of both pronunciation and articulation. The first word of the 3/4 bar is *hing*. The initial *h* is an aspirated sound that gets your air moving; the *ee* vowel that follows lends a bright quality; the buzzy *ng* focuses the sound even further. Observe the staccato so that there is space before you intone the vowel on beat 2 of each measure, and bring the focus of *hing* into the vowel. Notice that the vowel spectrum moves from closed to open: *ee-ay-eh-ah*.

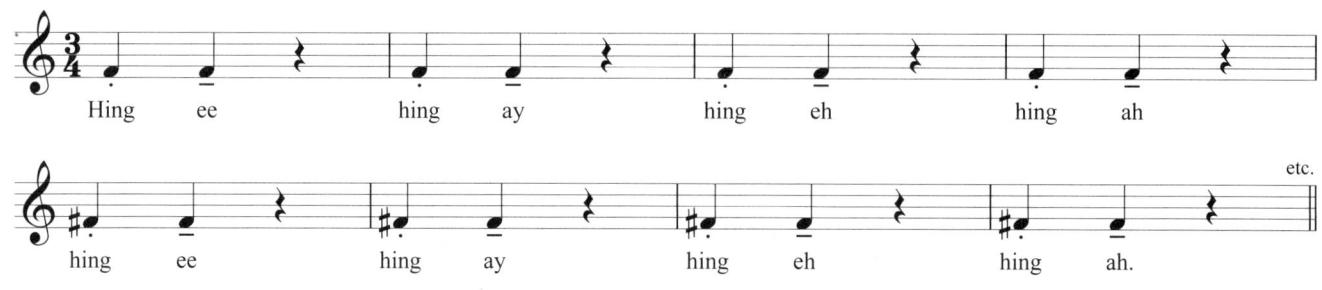

Extra: Repeat the exercise, ignoring the staccato on beat 1; sing from *ng* directly into the vowel that follows.

THU

Topic: Portamento up an octave

In Week 6, you were introduced to the portamento. Let's expand on that, singing an octave interval rather than a fifth. (First, review that one and read the instructions, page 15). Previously, we used a hum. Do that here, but also sing the vowels shown in the example below. Choose others as well.

FRI

Topic: Quick and easy warm-up

Today we'll sing an eighth-note arpeggio and a 16th-note scale. This versatile aerobic will animate your voice and breath quickly. It can be used in a variety of ways, allowing you to play with various vowels and articulations. First, sing the syllables shown below, starting slowing. Then experiment with staccato vs. legato, sing all on a single vowel, etc. Use your imagination!

SAT

Topics: Vocal freedom; warming up

This aerobic is so simple, but it feels so good! Articulate a lip trill as you slide up a fifth, then—as you descend—switch to the vowels shown below. Always be careful of the half step between mi-fa (or fa-mi, in this instance); it's easy to let it be slightly under pitch. After singing the indicated syllables, mix and match them as you like.

SUN

Topic: Register transition, head to chest

Practice moving from head voice down into the nether regions of chest voice. Singing at the notated pitch (not an octave lower, men), begin with a good owl-like sound on *hoo* and sing down the five-note scale. Keep it legato. Alternate *hoo* with *hee*. As you go lower, mix the two voices as you begin to engage chest voice. Eventually, you should be in pure chest voice.

VOCAL AEROBICS
WEEK 15

MON
Topic: Enunciation
First, listen to the demo track; the objectives and the way to proceed will become clear. Okay, so now you realize that we have not shown the entire etude in the printed music. We're singing up a major scale and back down again, using this tongue-twister. To quote the legendary choral conductor Robert Shaw, "Sing all the sounds of all the words." Yep, enunciate every little part of it, starting at a slow tempo. Increase the speed when you're ready.

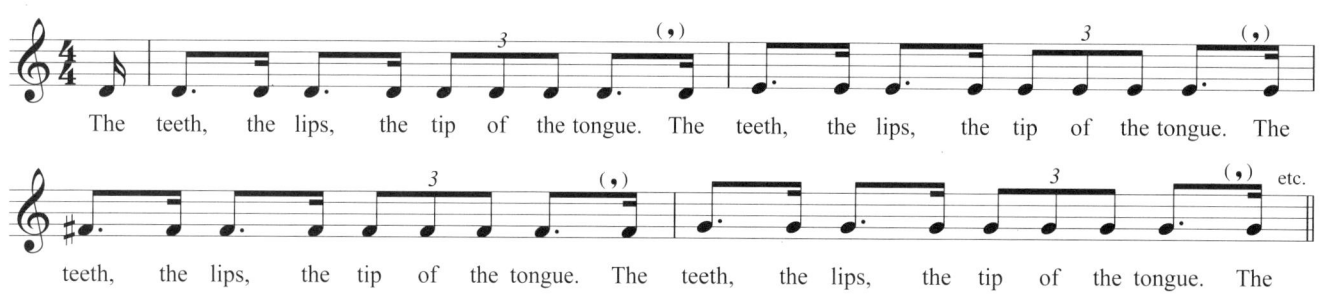

TUE
Topic: Consonant, M
We often use an initial *m* when singing vocal exercises. Why is that? Well, it's because the sound is essentially a hum, which is an excellent tool for focusing the sound. Your lips are pressed together gently, your tongue is relaxed and forward, and the air comes out of your nose. M is a voiced continuant consonant.

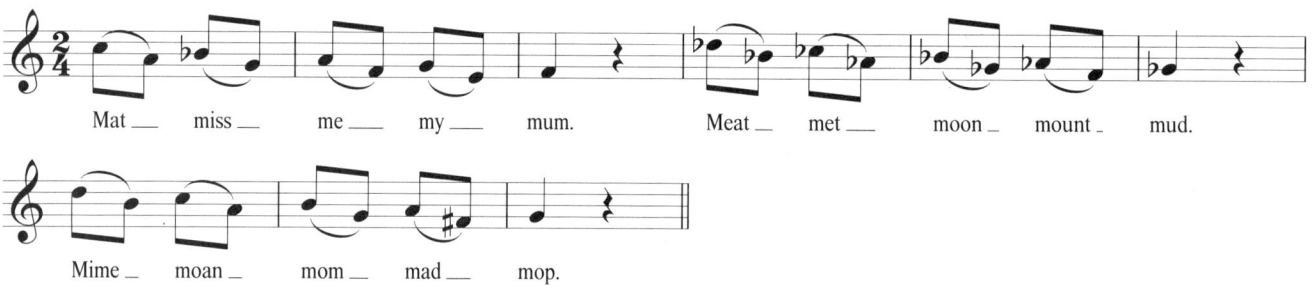

WED
Topics: Note accuracy; fourths
This exercise will test your ear and warm up your voice at the same time. A sequence of four ascending fourth intervals allows us to sing to from the starting note (root) up an octave. Notice that the penultimate note of each pattern is the leading tone, a half step below the octave. Always make sure to sing it in tune; you can feel its pull toward the final note. Practice first with detached syllables, then with a single legato vowel. Two suggestions are given in the example below; make up others on your own.

THU

Topic: OH-OO diphthong

Below are the first three notes of a minor scale. We'll use them to practice a new diphthong, singing "Oh no, don't go." What two vowel sounds do you hear in each of those words? (Remember, the first is sustained, the second is much quicker.) That's correct: *oh-oo*. Sing the notes and rhythms as indicated, breathing after each two-bar phrase. Listen to the demo first.

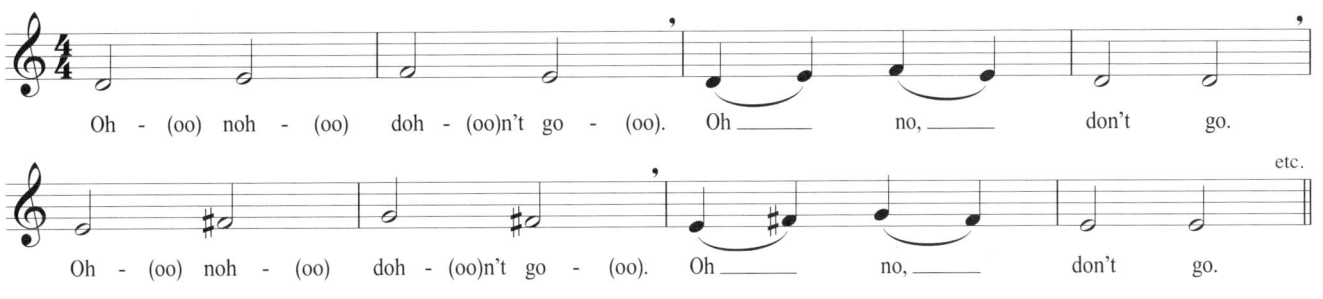

FRI

Topics: Diatonic melody; intervals

This diatonic melody is a good tool for practicing your intervals. It's set in C major, but you should sing it in other keys as well. Before adding the words, practice on a hum and on vowels of your choosing, always keeping a waltz-like lilt to the music. When you're ready for the text, put to good use all the hard work you've done on consonants and vowels.

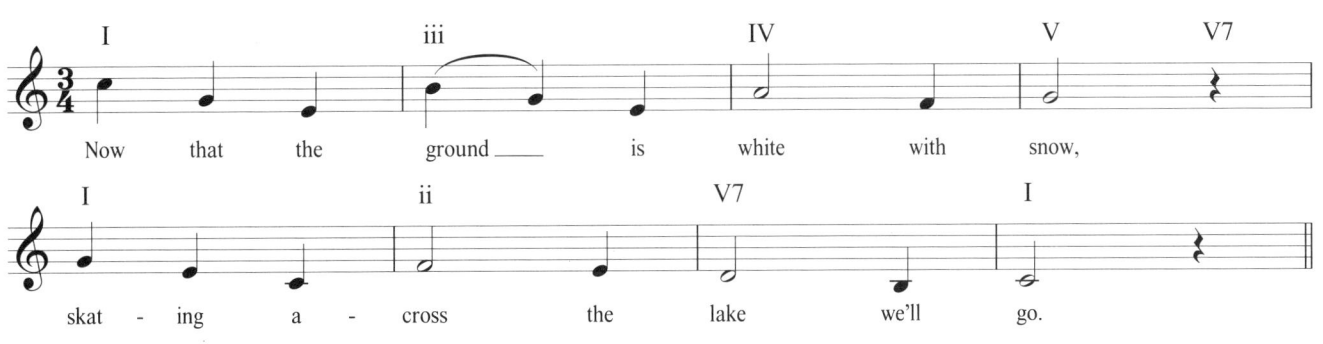

SAT

Topic: Pentatonic scale

As you might infer from its name, the *pentatonic scale* contains five notes. It is comprised of the first (*do*), second (*re*), third (*mi*), fifth (*sol*), and sixth (*la*) notes of the major scale. Though often utilized in folk music, hymns, and spirituals, it is also found in pop/rock music—for example, in Led Zeppelin's "Whole Lotta Love." Practice singing on the syllables shown below, first on each note, then as a longer phrase.

SUN

Topic: Auld Lang Syne; pentatonic scale

"Auld Lang Syne" is a pentatonic song that gets butchered every New Year's Eve. The title literally translates as "old long since," which basically means "days gone by." Practice the melody, first by humming, then by using syllables of your choosing. Now you're ready to add the words, penned by the Scottish poet Robert Burns. As you raise your glass in a toast at midnight on December 31, you can lead the singing—and you'll know just what it is you're singing about!

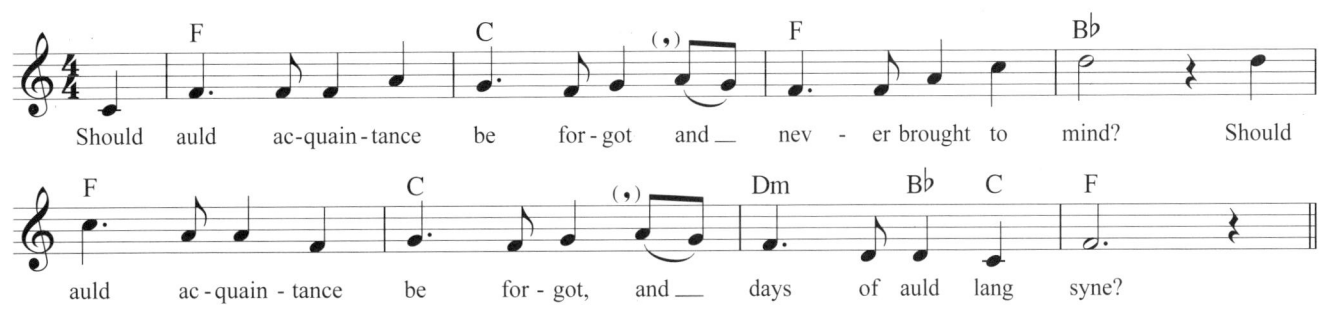

VOCAL AEROBICS
WEEK 16

Robert Burns, the national poet of Scotland, wrote this beautiful poem in 1791. The music was penned in 1837 by Jonathan Spilman, a Kentucky-born lawyer, minister, and sometime-composer. The melody's gentle shape and its soothing rhythm is a perfect match for Burns's poetic tribute to the River Afton.

Take a look at the sheet music on page 35. A recurring melodic pattern is an arpeggiated major chord. It's inverted, though, with the top note on the bottom. Listen to the demo track, then sing this simple exercise.

Now we'll expand on that a bit, singing the fifth of the major chord both on the bottom and the top of the arpeggio. Use good breath management and keep it legato. Tilt your head back a bit as you sing up and over, to make sure there's no tension in the throat.

Find the measures (23-24) with the words "yon thorny den." Let's practice that melodic pattern at several pitch levels. Notice that the first interval is a half-step down; there's also a half-step leading to bar 24. If we're not paying attention, we might tend to sing these a little flat; keep them accurately in tune. Crescendo across the three-bar phrase.

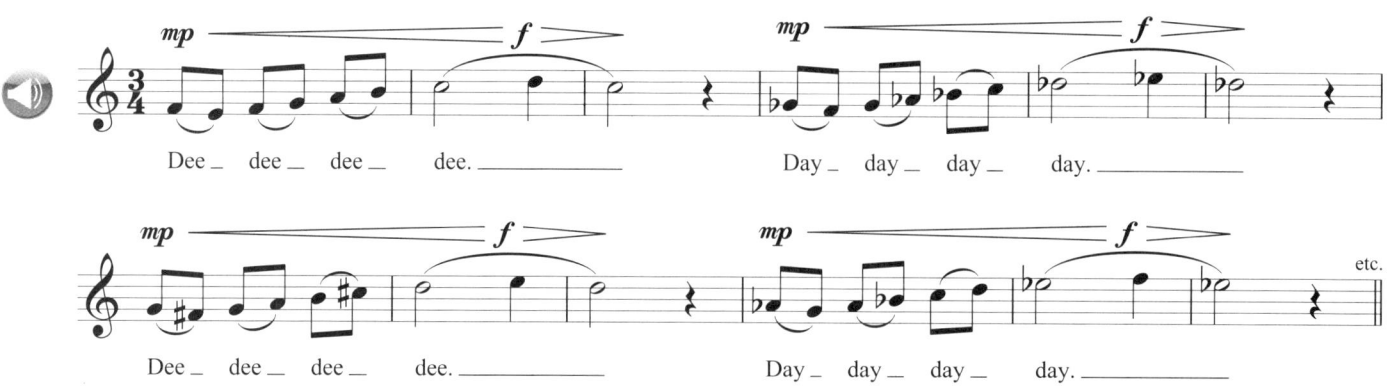

Remember to practice the song on a hum, on a lip trill, and on various vowels before you add the words. As is often the case with folksongs, this one divides into symmetrical four-bar phrases. That's a good way to tackle learning it, a little at a time. Ultimately, you'll want that phrase structure to order your breathing—every four measures, in other words. Enjoy!

Flow Gently, Sweet Afton

Words by ROBERT BURNS
Music by JONATHAN SPILMAN

VOCAL AEROBICS
WEEK 17

MON

Topics: Minor triad arpeggios, ascending/descending; compound meter
In Week 14, we sang major octave arpeggios in 6/8 time. Let's follow the same set of guidelines, but sing minor arpeggios instead. Listen to the online demo before you begin.

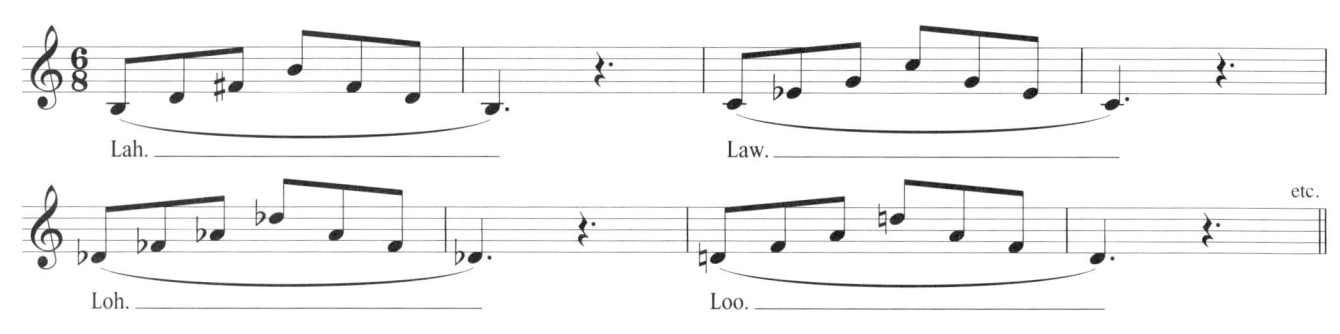

TUE

Topic: Strengthening the chest voice
Today, let's concentrate on strengthening the middle and lower parts of the voice. Sing a descending five-note scale on *ha*. Each pitch should be an accented staccato. Take it slowly, expanding your breathing muscles before every note; no throat tension allowed! Keep moving the pattern down by half steps until you have reached your lowest comfortable note.

WED

Topics: Vocal focus; dotted rhythm
This bizarre aerobic is useful for focusing your voice and your vowels. We're moving from a front, closed, bright vowel (*ee*) to an open, back, dark vowel (*ah*), employing a dotted rhythm and voiced consonants. Make sure the *ah* is open enough and, at the same time, well-focused. Give full rhythmic value to the tied quarter-notes.

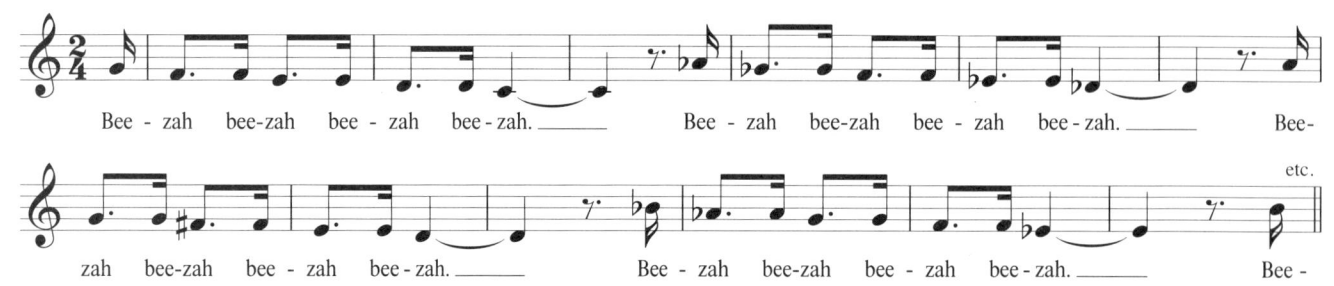

THU

Topic: Loosening up

Here is a fun way to get your breath and your lips moving. For the most part, we are singing an *ee* vowel. Keep it bright and make sure the voiced consonants *b* and *d* are on the same pitch as the vowels. At first, observe the eighth rests; as you become more facile, try singing each five-bar iteration in a single breath. Enjoy!

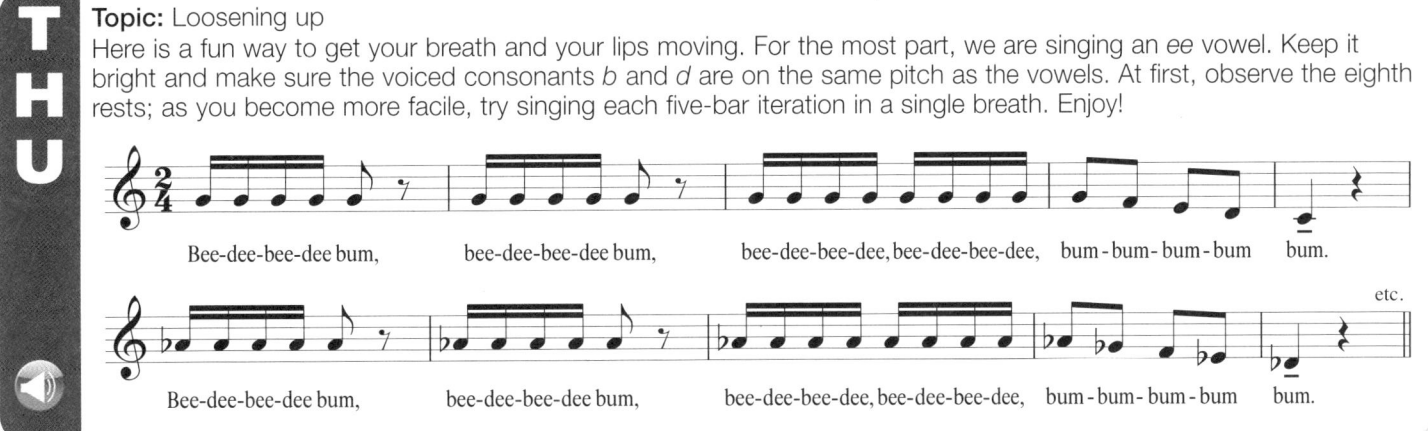

FRI

Topics: Intonation; flexibility

Today we use a five-note descending pattern and add some friendly neighbor tones to it. Start with a firm tone, breathing on the quarter rests. Your sound will tend to diminish as you descend the scale. Offset that by using your fast air, all the way through the three-beat note at the end of each phrase. Beware of the half steps between mi-fa and ti-do.

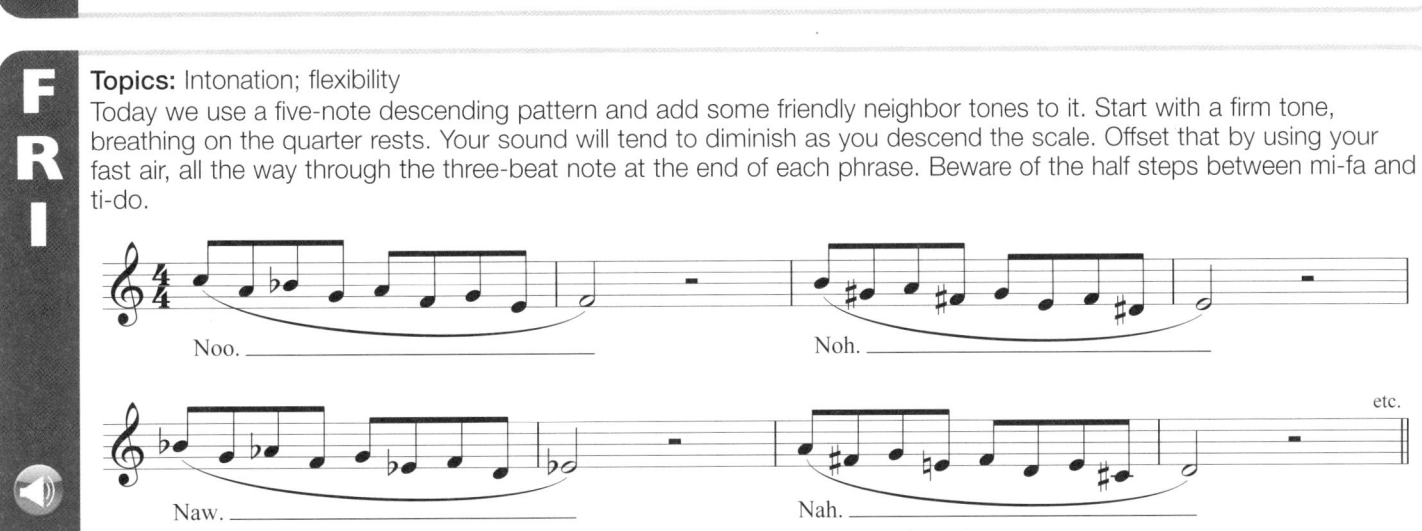

SAT

Topic: Register transition, head to chest

Let's expand on an etude from Week 14. We're still using a five-note scale, but now singing curly-cues around it in 6/8 meter. Start in head voice at the notated pitch, singing *noo*. Use the *n* to focus into the vowel. Begin to feel your chest voice engage as you go lower. At first, you will sense a mixture of the two registers, but eventually will move into chest-dominated sounds. Repeat the process by singing *nee*. Listen to the demo first.

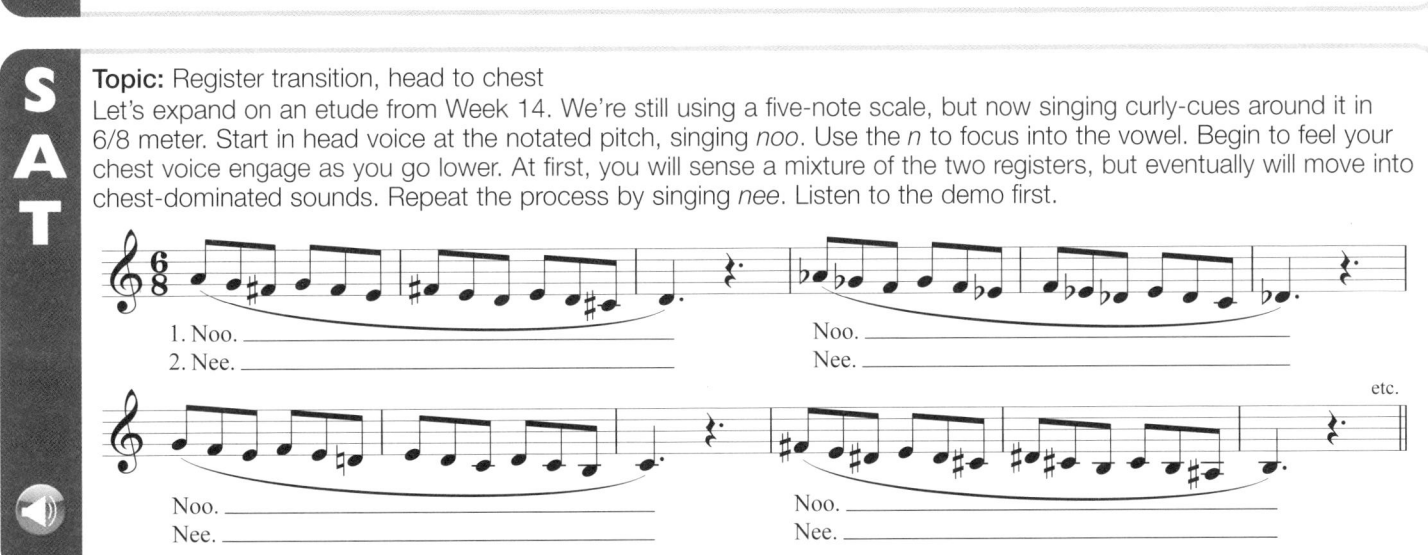

SUN

Topic: Consonants, S & Z

S and *z* are close cousins. Both are continuant consonants and are articulated in the same manner. Raise the tip of your tongue toward the center of your upper front teeth, but don't let it touch them. The sides of your tongue should touch your upper side teeth. The only difference is that *s* is voiceless and *z* is voiced. (*S* is also called a *sibilant*, which simply means it makes a hissing sound.) In the etude below, notice that each successive two-bar iteration is a whole step lower.

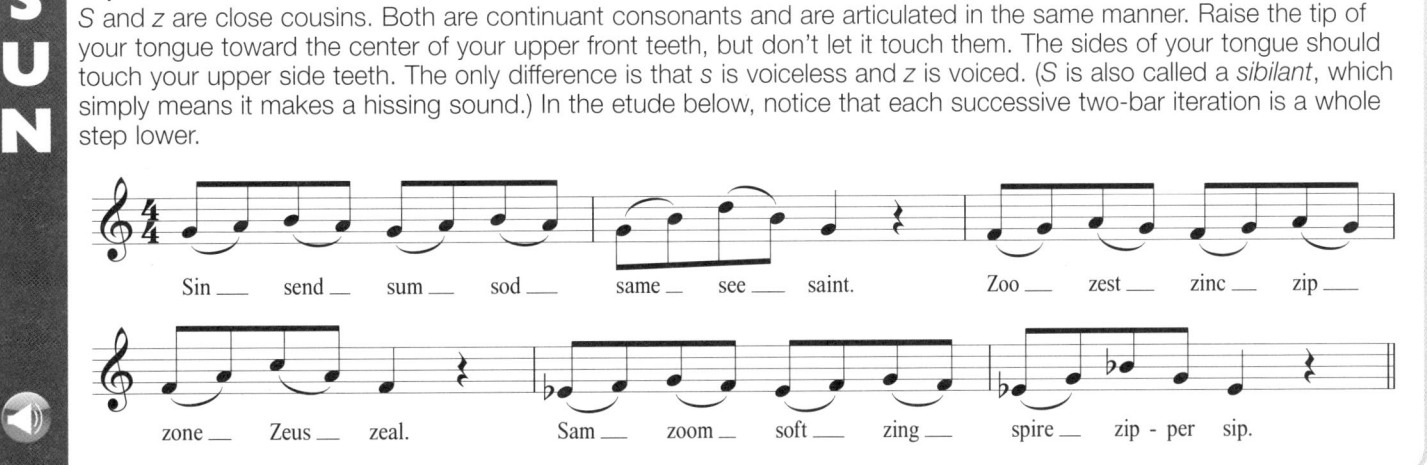

VOCAL AEROBICS — WEEK 18

MON

Topic: Flexibility

Practice this etude three ways, as indicated in the music example below. First, sing a syllable on each note, then on each beat, then on each phrase. Our aim here is to sing flexibly and evenly as we ascend the five-note scale and its neighbor tones. Go slowly at first, increasing the tempo across several days of practice.

1. Dee dee dee dee dee dee dee dee dee dee dee dee dee   Dee dee dee dee dee dee dee dee dee dee dee dee
2. Doo ____ doh ____ daw ____ dah. _____   Doo ____ doh ____ daw ____ dah. _____
3. Deh. _____   Deh. _____

TUE

Topic: Singing thirds and fourths

Today's vocalise takes one from Week 15 a bit further. Alternating ascending fourths with descending thirds, we traverse the interval of a tenth (octave + third). On the way back down, we reverse the procedure, singing descending fourths and ascending thirds. This is an effective way to work on pitch acuity across a wide range. Sing staccato—and use your keyboard to check your accuracy.

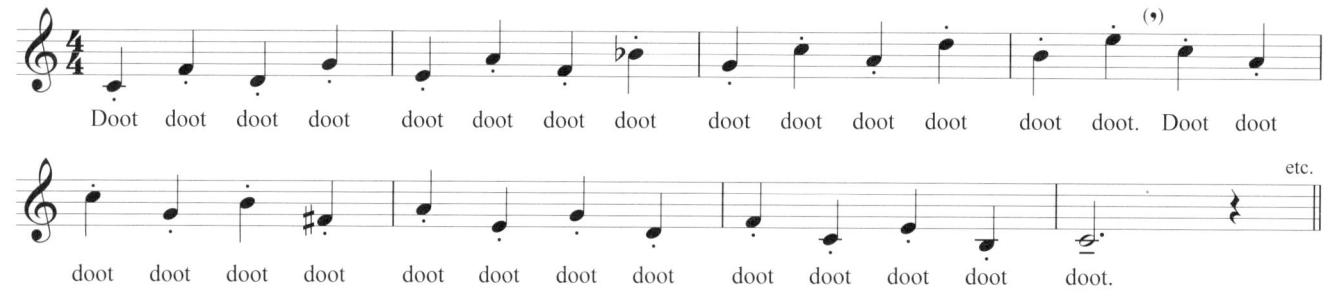

Doot doot doot doot doot doot doot doot doot doot doot doot doot. Doot doot
doot doot doot doot doot doot doot doot doot doot doot doot.

WED

Topic: Diphthongs with schwa [ə]

Across the past several weeks, we have learned about five different diphthongs. (See pages 13, 22, 25, 28, and 33.) To that knowledge, let's add a few more. These will employ the neutral vowel that linguists call a *schwa*. We notate it like this: [ə]. It is an unaccented sound, as in the last syllable of "father." Say "father." You didn't say "fah-their," did you? Of course not! That final neutral vowel is the schwa: [ə]. Say "air." Did you pronounce the final *r*? Nope! That's a schwa, combined with an initial *eh* sound: eh-[ə]. As with the other diphthongs, sustain the first vowel sound and add the second vowel (schwa) at the very end.

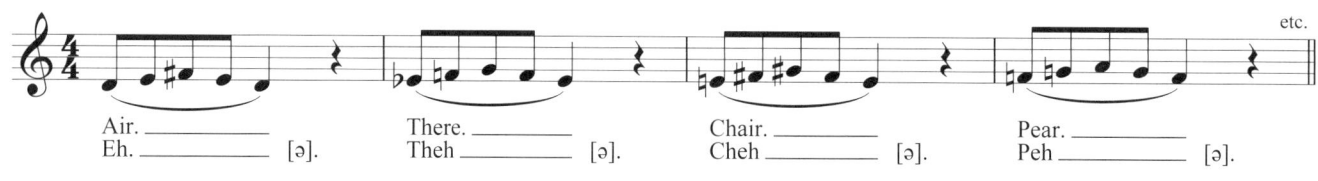

Air. _____   There. _____   Chair. _____   Pear. _____
Eh. _____ [ə].   Theh _____ [ə].   Cheh _____ [ə].   Peh _____ [ə].

THU

Topic: Diphthongs with schwa [ə], continued

Now that you've got the hang of it, we can easily learn three more. Say: "ear, ore, poor." If you break those down, you'll hear that the sounds are *ih*-[ə], *aw*-[ə], and *poo*-[ə]. Remember: There's no final *r* sound, the first vowel is sustained, and the neutral schwa is added at the last second. Try these. Notice that we're using the first three notes of the minor scale this time.

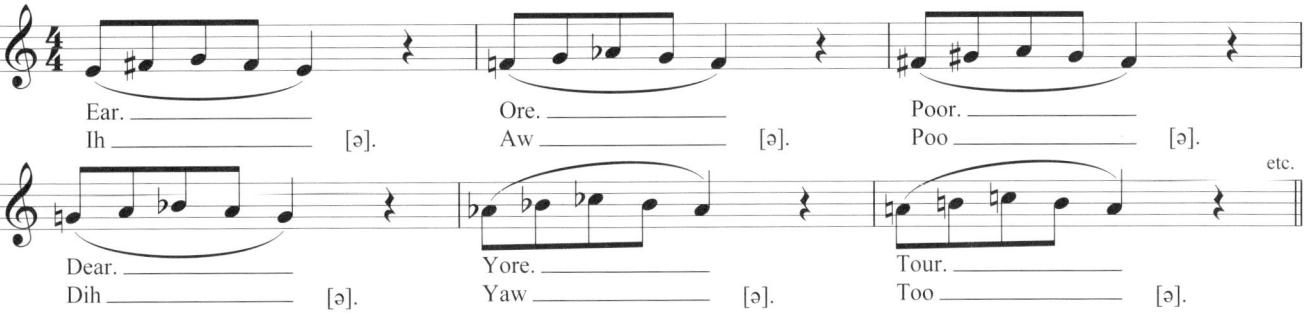

FRI

Topics: Dynamics; breath management

If you need a quick refresher course on dynamics, look back to Week 8 ("All Through the Night"). We're going to start very quietly, using our back and abdominal muscles to breathe on each rest in bars 1 and 2, and increasing the volume as we proceed. We sing bar 3 in a single breath, observing the dynamics as marked. Alternate the vowels as indicated.

SAT

Topic: Minor-key melody (hymn tune: "Morning Song")

Sometimes it's fun to vocalize on a "real" tune—or even part of one. This minor-key melody (notice the key signature) is an early American folk hymn. It dates back at least to the early 19th century, and probably is even older than that. It was included in a collection called *Wyeth's Repository of Sacred Music* (1813), and has been sung to various texts. We've indicated some syllables, but mix and match your own as well. Sing molto legato.

SUN

Topics: Warming up; getting the breath moving

Remember the silly aerobic from Week 7? (See page 17.) Yes, that one. Read the instructions and sing it a few times before practicing today's warm-up. The same concepts apply, though now we're coving a ninth instead of a fifth. Crescendo, and feel your air speed up, as you ascend to the top notes. The sound will tend to diminish as you descend, but use good support to keep it strong. No throat muscles allowed!

VOCAL AEROBICS
WEEK 19

MON

Topic: Five-note scale; three-note scale

This simple aerobic combines two familiar patterns, the descending five-note major scale and the three-note scale. Breathe low and keep the sound supported as you move across the phrase, molto legato. We've indicated a few vowels, but you should sing others of your choosing as well.

Nih. _____ Neh. _____

Nah. _____

TUE

Topic: Balanced onset

Before you practice today's aerobic, look back at Week 14. This one also encourages a balanced onset, with an attack that is not too hard and not breathy. Inhale on each quarter rest. As before, if the initial *h* causes you to run out of breath, omit it; be careful not to use a glottal stop, though.

Hoh hoh hoh hoh hoh hoh hoh hoh hoh hoh hoh hoh hoh.

Hoh hoh hoh hoh hoh hoh hoh hoh hoh hoh hoh hoh hoh.

Hoh hoh hoh hoh hoh hoh hoh hoh hoh hoh hoh hoh hoh.

WED

Topics: Range extension; vowel purity

Remember our friends, the octave arpeggios? Let's pay them a visit. There are a couple of objectives here. One is range extension, moving higher; the other is maintaining vowel consistency. We begin with a focused, closed vowel, leap up an octave, then descend the arpeggio on *ah*. Use fast air as the closed vowel catapults you into the *ah*; tilt to your head back slightly, to avoid any neck tension. Be sure to keep your throat open, your soft palate raised, and the back of your tongue down. Listen for a nice, spacious, beautiful sound. "Ahhh…"

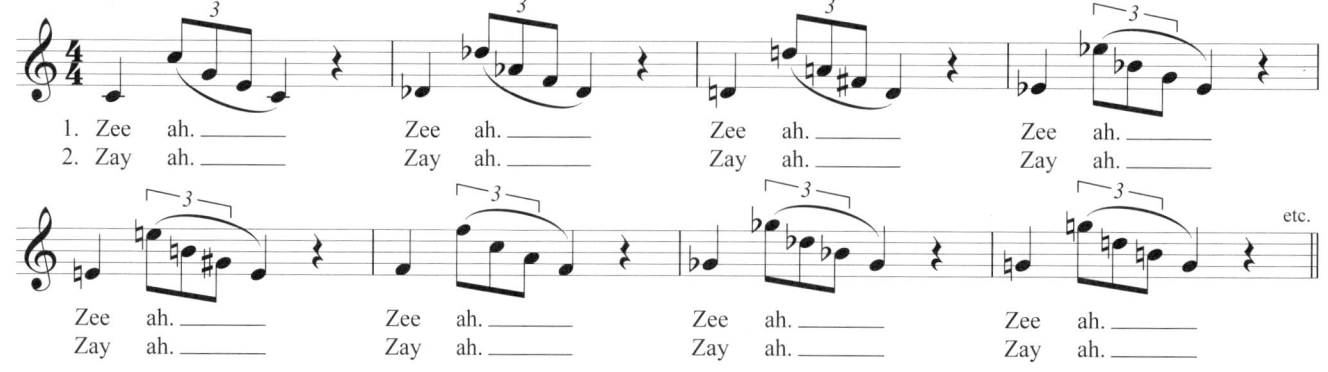

1. Zee ah. Zee ah. Zee ah. Zee ah.
2. Zay ah. Zay ah. Zay ah. Zay ah.

Zee ah. Zee ah. Zee ah. Zee ah.
Zay ah. Zay ah. Zay ah. Zay ah.

THU

Topics: Musical accuracy; expressivity

Let us sing a new melody to reinforce several concepts: pitch accuracy, rhythmic acuity, expressivity, well-enunciated consonants, and well-shaped vowel sounds. You will notice that there are tied notes, dotted rhythms, words with several notes, and stepwise motion as well as leaping intervals. With a pencil, write in dynamic marks, phrasing, and crescendo/diminuendo. Before singing the words, practice on *dee*, *deh*, and *dah*.

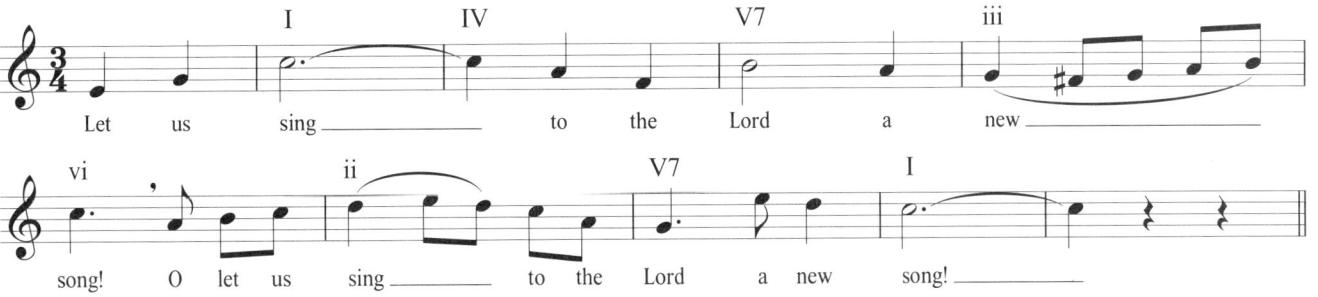

FRI

Topics: Relaxed jaw; legato; low range

Today's exercise uses elements of both the triad arpeggio and the five-note scale. It begins in the middle of your voice, but take it as low as you comfortably can, moving down by half steps. Keep your jaw loose and relaxed, singing the two-note phrases legato, with slight emphasis on the first note of each. Be sure to keep the *ah* nice and rich as you go lower. Think dark chocolate.

SAT

Topics: Breath; legato; crescendo

Like the three-note scale we saw in Week 6, this is a good aerobic to place near the beginning of your warm-up time. It's an ascending five-note major scale preceded by repeated whole steps. Those first two beats of each iteration are sort of like revving your motor before driving up a gentle incline. Feel your breath speed increase as your move through the phrase and keep the dotted-half note well supported. Use the syllables as notated, then mix it up for yourself.

SUN

Topic: Breath; legato; diminuendo

Today's exercise is similar to yesterday's, but this time we're singing down the five-note scale. Use a well-focused hum on the first iteration, then a vowel, then a hum, etc. To get started, sing the *mee* and *may* syllables as shown, then add others: *meh*, *moh*, *maw*, *mah*.

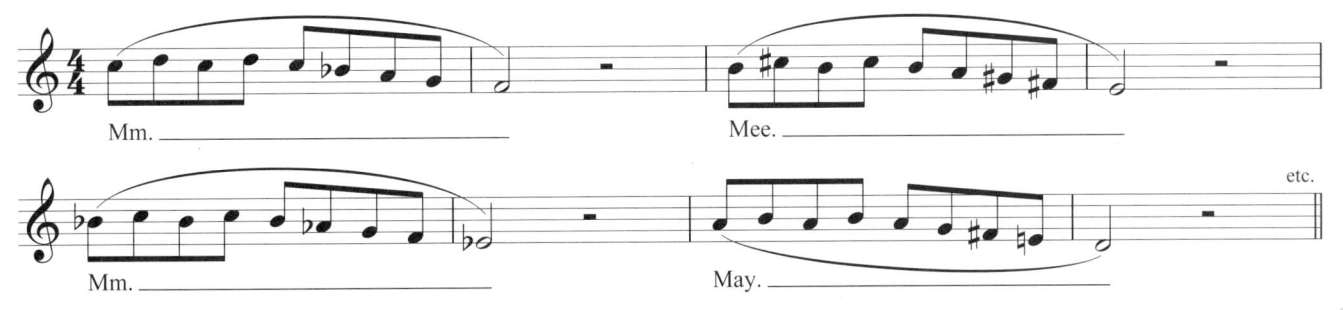

VOCAL AEROBICS — WEEK 20

MON

Topics: Breath management; intonation; flexibility

Let's stick with the familiar five-note scale, but elaborate on it just a bit. We have several goals in mind here: efficient breath management, accurate intonation, vocal flexibility, and an expressive shape to each phrase. Take a good, low breath on each quarter rest. As you move up and over the melodic pattern, feel the exhalation speed just a bit to affect a crescendo. Be sure to hold the dotted-half note for three full counts. We've given some suggestions about what sounds to sing, but you can just as easily choose your own!

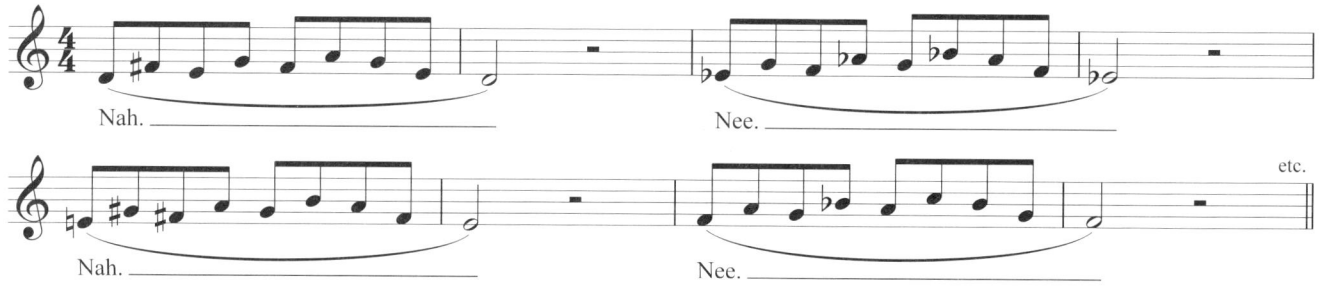

TUE

Topics: Open-to-closed-to-open vowels; major triads

Today's aerobic takes its inspiration from the one we sang in Week 5. Review that one. Let's flip it over and also sing a set of vowels, this time from open to closed to open. As before, sing with the initial consonants, then just with the vowels. What did you do physically to achieve this?

WED

Topic: Falsetto/head voice

In most of these aerobics, you gentlemen are singing an octave lower than the notated pitch—since all are in the treble clef. Not so in this instance. Today's etude is designed to help both women and men move from head voice (men: falsetto) to chest voice. Begin the exercise in head voice, then, as you move down by half steps, allow the voices to mix. Keep going until you are completely in chest voice. Mixing legato and staccato articulations is quite effective here. Listen to the demo before you sing.

42

THU

Topic: Singing expressively

"Come All Ye Fair and Tender Maidens" is a folksong from Kentucky. It is only eight bars long, but there are seven verses. (You can find the whole song online or in *The Big Book of Folksongs*, HL00312549.) Listen to the expressive performance of verse 1 on the demo track, then use the backing track to sing it yourself. The playback feature allows you to change the key, so experiment with several to find the one most comfortable for you.

FRI

Topics: Breath management; octave leap; descending octave scale

This useful exercise highlights several concepts simultaneously: breath management, crescendo, diminuendo, dynamics, octave leaps, flexibility, etc. Begin softly and crescendo through the octave leap and across the five-beat tied notes. Move seamlessly into the eighth notes and descend the major scale; as always, beware of the half steps between ti-do and mi-fa. Give the dotted-half note three full counts. The music example uses *loh* and *lah*, but you should practice with other vowels as well.

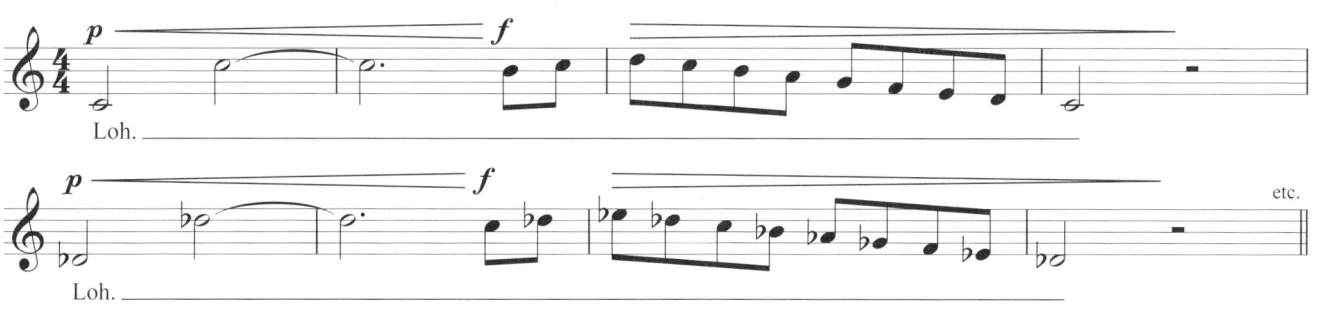

SAT

Topics: Minor five-note scale; 16th notes; leading tones; flexibility

Remember that the only difference between the five-note major scale and the minor is that the third note is a half-step lower. Let's practice that on a couple of 16th-note iterations, then add the lower leading tone at the end, singing eighth notes. This etude is good for practicing vocal flexibility and for working on pitch acuity. Begin at a tempo that allows you to sing each note accurately, increasing the speed over time.

SUN

Topic: Extending and strengthening the lower range

If you've ever sung in a choir, your director may have used vocalises with words such as "I love to sing"—or like the one below, in which the text painting is obvious. Sing the slurred notes molto legato, with well-articulated consonants and beautifully shaped vowels. (Listen to the demo.) Continue moving down by half-steps, all the way to your lowest comfortable notes; "go today" should be rich and full.

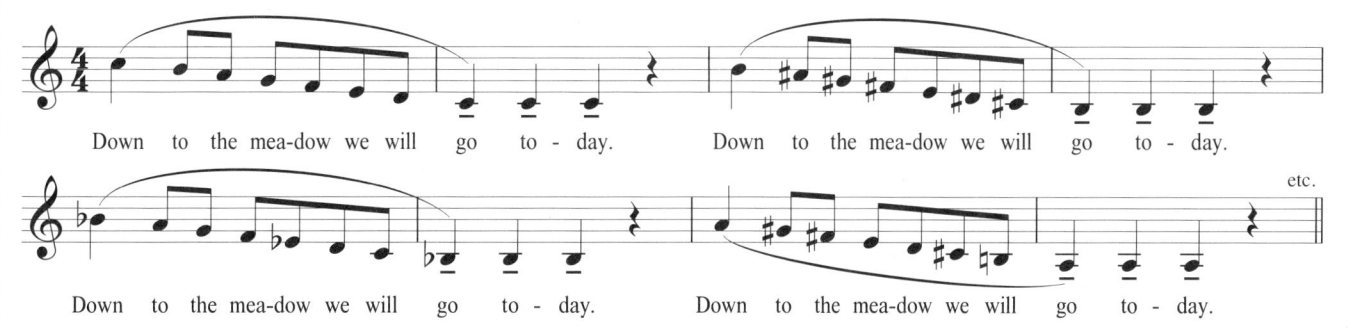

VOCAL AEROBICS
WEEK 21

MON

Topics: Portamento; minor triad; warm-up

Using a portamento to slide down and up a perfect fifth and to outline a minor triad will warm up both your voice and your ears. Listen for accurate intonation, especially on the middle note of the minor chord. Take it slowly, using a hum, lip roll, and vowels of your choosing.

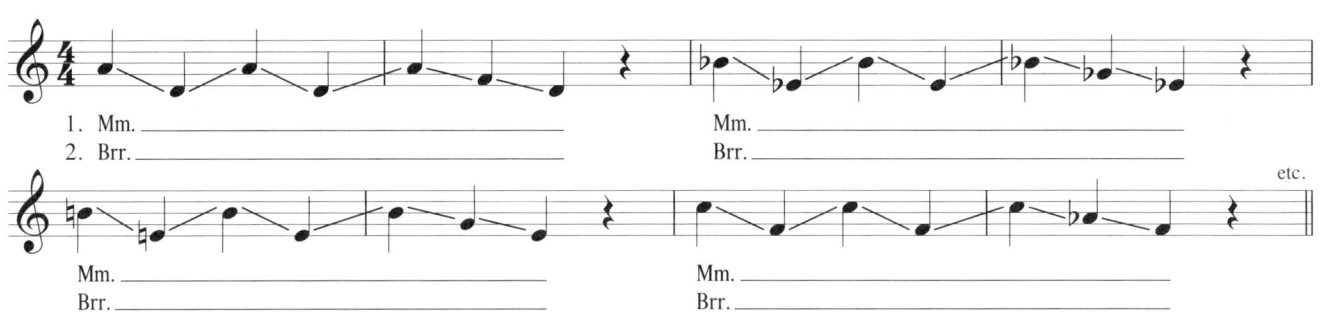

TUE

Topics: Octave scale, descending; articulation

Remember our old buddy, the octave scale? Today we're going to sing that familiar pattern, but mix it up a bit. We're in 5/4 meter, with both staccato and legato articulations. Use a firm forte throughout, allowing good breath support to offset the natural tendency to diminuendo as you descend.

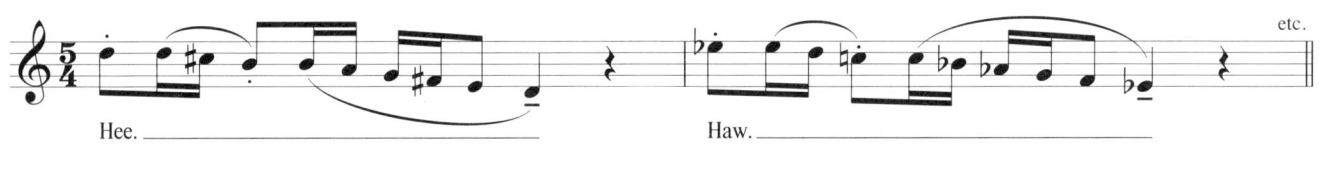

WED

Topic: Singing accurately and expressively

This wistful little folksong comes from Tennessee. "Cotton Eyed Joe" is only eight bars long, and you'll notice that measures 5-8 are exactly like measures 1-4. Sing the gentle syncopations in bars 1, 3, 5, and 7 accurately and expressively. There are separate demo and piano accompaniment tracks for this song included in the online audio.

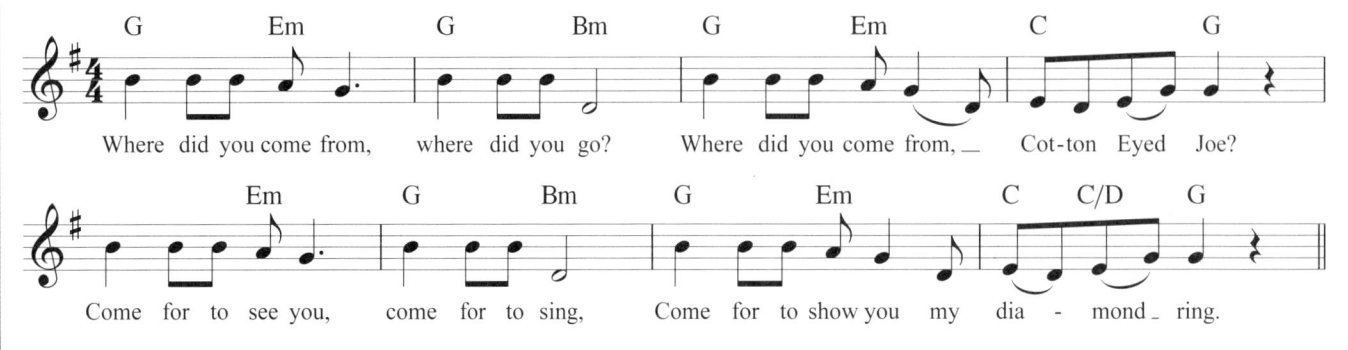

THU

Topic: Falsetto for men

Gentlemen, this falsetto-strengthening aerobic is specifically for you, but the ladies are welcome to try it, too. Begin at the notated pitch, not an octave below. (Listen to the demo!) Take it slowly, bouncing your diaphragm as you pulse staccato eighth notes on *hoo*. Stay in falsetto until it breaks on the bottom. Do not mix your chest voice into the sound.

Hoo hoo hoo hoo   hoo hoo hoo hoo   hoo.   Hoo hoo hoo hoo   hoo hoo hoo hoo   hoo.   Hoo hoo hoo hoo   hoo hoo hoo hoo   hoo.

Hoo hoo hoo hoo   hoo hoo hoo hoo   hoo.   Hoo hoo hoo hoo   hoo hoo hoo hoo   hoo.   etc.

FRI

Topic: Consonants K & G

The consonants *k* and *g* are stop-plosives. (See Week 13.) They are created in a similar manner, with the back of the tongue raised against the soft palate and the tip of the tongue forward. For *k*, drop your tongue quickly and send your breath out plosively; for *g*, drop your tongue quickly and emit a vocal sound plosively. (This *g* is sometimes referred to as a hard *g*, as opposed to the *soft g* in a word like "George.")

King   keep   kale   ken   kick   cup   cat.   Got   gill   glove   game   go   Grinch   gal.

Clap   gig   kink   good   keel   gun   kraut.   Get   cop   great   core   gut   croon   grass.

SAT

Topics: Sixths ascending, fifths descending; pitch accuracy; intervals

As we progress further in our studies, we want to continue to challenge ourselves vocally, aurally, and musically. In previous weeks, we have practiced singing intervals, beginning with the narrower ones and expanding incrementally. Today, let's add another set. Move up the scale intoning ascending sixths and descending fifths. Reverse the process on the way down. Sing *tah* as shown in the music example, then add syllables of your own choosing. Use your keyboard to keep you on the right track.

Tah   tah   tah   tah   tah   tah   tah   tah   tah   tah.   Tah   tah   tah   tah   tah   tah   tah   tah   tah   tah   etc.

SUN

Topic: Mixing it up, diphthongs

Okay! The exercise below is a hodge-podge of words that utilize diphthongs. It's up to you to figure them out. Above the staff, write in the two vowel sounds for each. (Use a pencil, never ink.) Remember that, in a two-note phrase, the first note gets slightly more emphasis than the second.

Night,   day,   boy,   now,   no.   Woe,   thou,   toy,   fate,   kind.

Hair,   fear,   more,   pure,   cow.   Wake,   vow,   sow,   rare,   four.

Vocal Aerobics — WEEK 22

MON

Topic: Energizing voice and breath using vibrant consonants

Vibrant consonants like *z* and *ng* are great for energizing your breath and your voice. Ensure that the *ah* vowels are nice and rich—especially as you descend the arpeggio. First practice using the eighth rests as shown, then progress to singing two-bar phrases. Keep it animated!

Zing-a-zing-a zah, zing-a-zing-a zah, zing-a-zing-a zah. Zing-a-zing-a zah, zing-a-zing-a zah, zing-a-zing-a zah. Zing-a-zing-a zah, zing-a-zing-a zah, zing-a-zing-a zah. etc.

TUE

Topic: Singing across the register break, women and men

Here is a pattern you've seen before: an octave scale, ascending then descending. This time we're going use it as a means of singing across the register break (head voice; chest voice). In the example below, we show D to D; find the places in your voice where it works best. Women probably will want to start lower than D; men may wish to start higher. For the ascending scale, start firmly in your chest voice and, as you go higher, feel the transition to head voice. Coming down, start in head voice and reverse the process. Keep it healthy and avoid any throat constriction. In addition to *ah*, use the lip trill and other vowels, as you like.

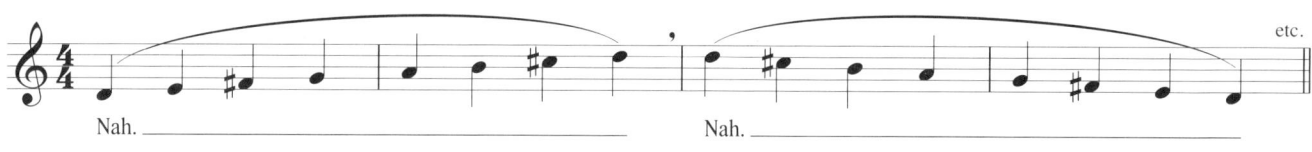

Nah. Nah. etc.

WED

Topic: Consonants SH & ZH

Sh and *zh* are akin to each other. They are continuant consonants and are shaped the same way. Raise the tip of your tongue slightly higher than for *s*, toward the center of your upper front teeth. The sides of your tongue should be placed against the edges of your upper side teeth. The only difference is that *sh* is voiceless, so emit the breath forcefully, and *zh* is voiced, so engage your vocal cords. (Like *s*, *sh* is a sibilant.)

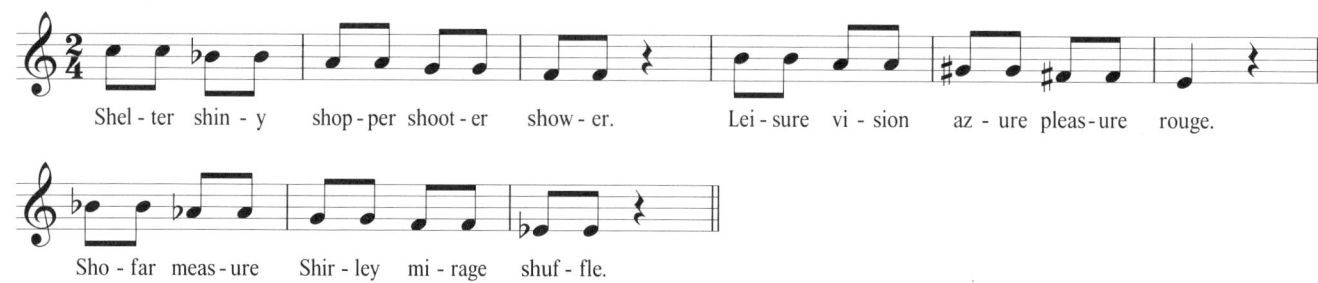

Shel-ter shin-y shop-per shoot-er show-er. Lei-sure vi-sion az-ure pleas-ure rouge.

Sho-far meas-ure Shir-ley mi-rage shuf-fle.

THU

Topic: Waltz; phrase shape; legato

The waltz was the most popular ballroom dance of the 19th century. Its gently lilting quality led any number of composers to take up the form—in ballets, operas, and instrumental music. Here's a little eight-bar waltz that allows us opportunity not only to practice singing over the range of an octave—both ascending and descending—but also to hone our musicality. Give emphasis to each downbeat (beat 1), and let the others glide past. The feel should be one beat to the bar, not three. Sing on *loo* and other vowels before adding the words.

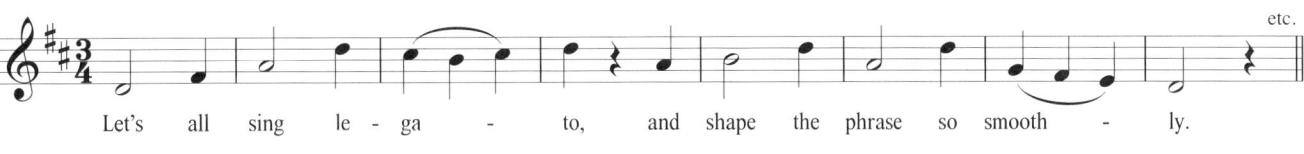

FRI

Topics: Dynamics; breath management

Here's our good friend, the five-note major scale. Let's enlist its help in practicing dynamics and good breath support. Replicate exactly what you see in the example below, alternating forte and piano in bar 1, then singing a diminuendo in bar 2.

SAT

Topic: Flexibility

Today's aerobic builds on an exercise we practiced in Week 18. Review that one and re-read its instructions. This time, we're ascending an octave, rather than a fifth. At first, you may need to catch a breath along the way. That's fine. The ultimate aim is to sing the entire phrase in a single breath. Move up/down by half steps to cover your current comfortable range.

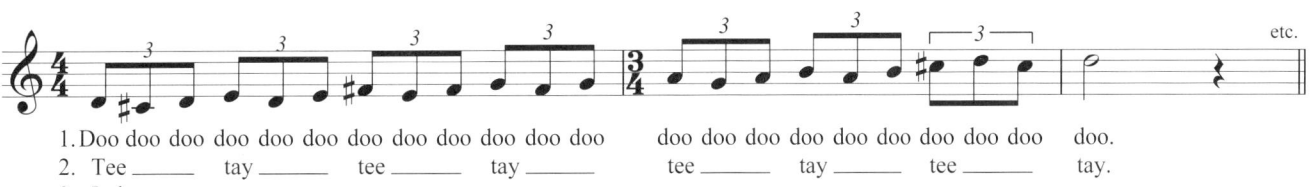

SUN

Topic: Register transition

This register transition exercise is for both women and men, to be sung at the notated pitches, starting on middle C. We begin with a sound that is predominantly chest voice, moving up a half-step after every two bars. As we go higher, we want to bring more head voice into the sound. *Oo* and *oh* are useful vowels here, but feel free to employ others if they work better for you. Exercise caution when practicing this aerobic: In singing, pain *never* equals gain, so if you feel any tension in your throat, stop and save this for another day.

Tip: Tilting your head back gently will help prevent any tendency to engage your neck muscles.

VOCAL AEROBICS — WEEK 23

MON
Topics: Breathing; dynamics; balanced onset; vowels

Ah! The descending five-note major scale! Let's use it to practice breathing, dynamics, balanced onset, and vowel sounds. After each eighth-note, replenish the tiny bit of air you expended. Alternate forte/piano and *lah/loo*; notice that singing *loo* makes the soft sound easier to manage because it is a closed vowel. The tenuto markings are to remind you to give full value to every note.

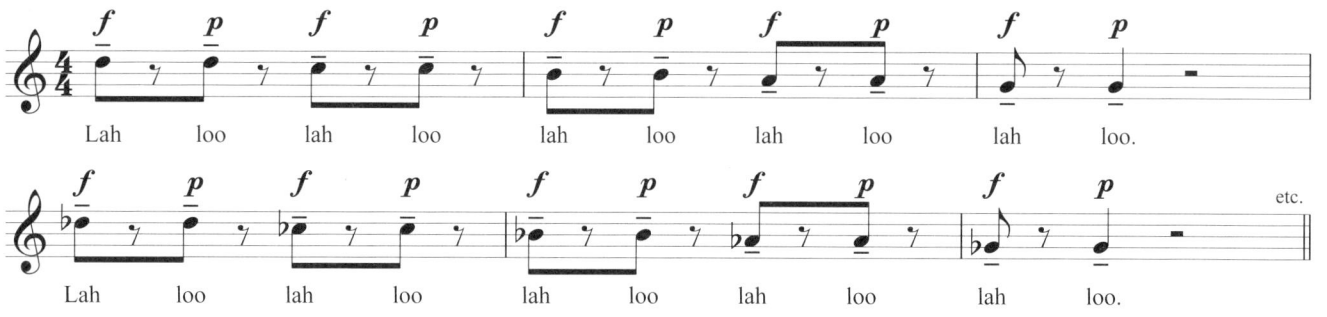

TUE
Topics: Molto legato, molto espressivo; minor key

Our goal today is to sing molto legato and molto espressivo. Oftentimes, these two objectives go hand-in-hand! We're in the key of G minor—a tonality Mozart used when he really wanted to turn on the pathos!—singing snippets of a 16th-century French melody. Strive for two four-bar phrases, but use the optional breaths as needed. Take note of the descending octave leap near the end; gauge your breath pressure accordingly.

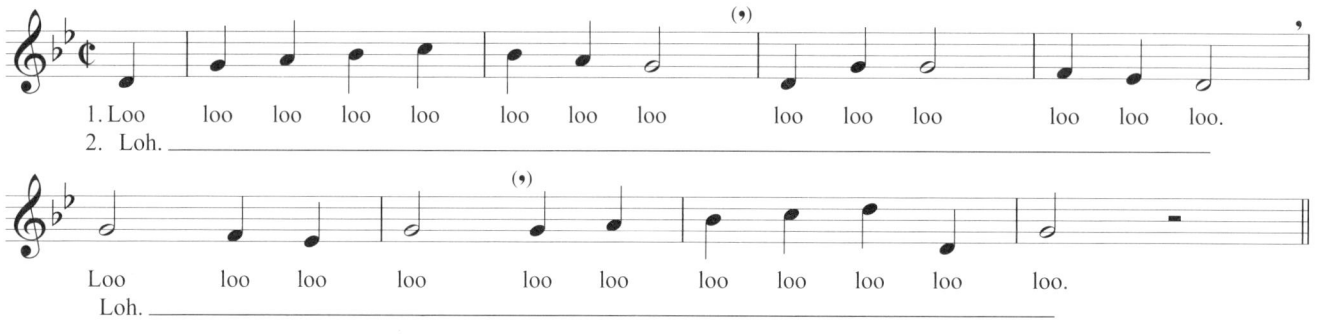

WED
Topics: Flexibility; even sound

Let's work toward flexibility and an even sound as we sing triplet patterns up the major scale, then come back down again. You'll need faster air as you ascend; gauge the breath pressure as you descend. Keep it legato, singing the syllables shown. Don't be intimidated by the changing time signatures in the printed music: The quarter note still gets the beat.

48

Topic: More falsetto for men

As we've noted previously, it's important to develop both vocal registers. Here is another falsetto exercise for the men. Essentially, we're outlining a descending arpeggio using our best cuckoo-like sound. (Listen to the demo.) Make sure the two even-eighths are staccato and that the quarter note gets its full value. Sing only in falsetto, stopping when the sound breaks. No chest voice for this one.

Topic: Singing sixths and sevenths

Have you noticed that, in our interval aerobics, the wider the interval, the shorter the etude? The obvious reason is that it takes less time to cover the same ground, so to speak. The interval of a seventh can sometimes be an awkward challenge. Sixths, both ascending and descending are more common and can be quite expressive in the context of a song. By now, you know the drill: sing accurately, using a piano to help you along. *Bim* and *tah* are good syllables for this one.

Topic: Singing over the register break

Like so many other vocal exercises, this one may seem a bit silly—but that doesn't make it any less effective! Here, we want to imitate a meowing cat as we sing across the register break. Both men and women should sing in the notated octave. As you incite the initial *m*, feel the lips buzz, then keep that as you move through the *ee* and the other sounds. Observe the crescendo/diminuendo marks and keep the tone a bit twangy.

Topics: Singing expressively; how to practice

This lilting little melody in 6/8 time is perfect for practicing legato, phrase shape, and expressivity. Note the use of crescendo and diminuendo "hair pins" and sing accordingly. Before trying the words, first practice with a hum, then with vowels of your choosing. Listen to the demo track.

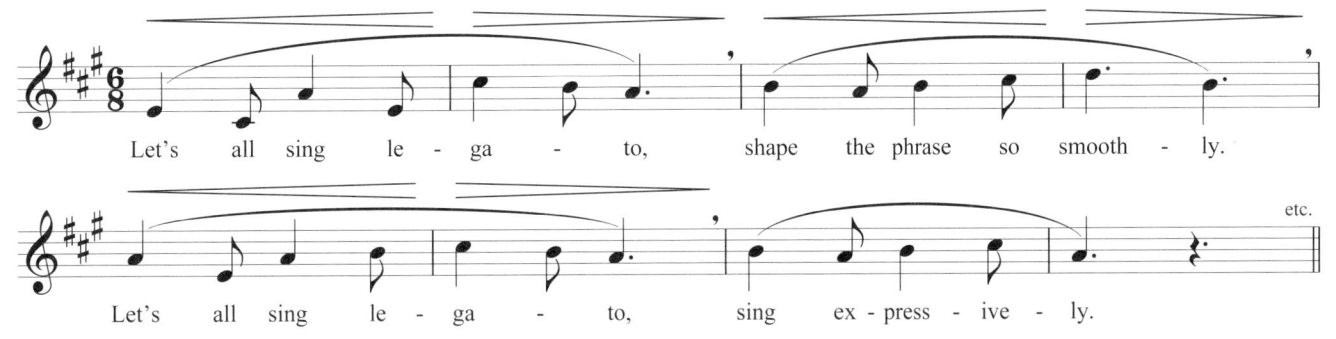

VOCAL AEROBICS
WEEK 24

Let's work on a holiday song! Everyone has their favorite Christmas carols, and this one ranks at the top of my list. The genesis of this universally beloved hymn dates back centuries and is shrouded in mystery. Latin was its original language, and you can still hear it sung way—by Bing Crosby, Nat King Cole, and others: "Adeste, fideles, Laeti, triumphantes…"

The English translation we sing nowadays was written by Frederick Oakeley, a 19th-century priest who lived and worked in the United Kingdom. There are quite a few verses—some hymnals have six or more!—but we have included only two. Feel free to consult other sources, printed or online, for the additional texts.

What adjectives would you use to describe this carol? Sturdy? Vigorous? Hopeful? Joyful? Do you have specific memories associated with it? Singing around the family piano? Caroling in the neighborhood? Going to church on Christmas Eve? These are questions to consider, because the answers may influence the way you choose to interpret the music and the feelings it may induce.

Though the song has been arranged in every musical style imaginable, there's something about a straightforward, pipe-organ-and-choir approach that seems especially appropriate. No vocal riffs on this one! The range is exactly one octave, so find the key that's most comfortable and you'll have no problems that way. (The lead sheet shows G major.)

Look at the music on page 51. Notice that there are some leaps in the first couple of bars, but after that, the vocal line is largely stepwise motion. Let's sing a few short exercises before working on the song itself.

Those leaps in bar 1 are the interval of a fourth. Sing a few for practice.

Bar 2 has a downward leap of a fifth. Practice that interval, followed by stepwise motion.

Sing these scales legato, breathing as indicated. Offset the natural tendency to get softer as you descend. Keep the sound full and strong.

O Come, All Ye Faithful

Words by JOHN FRANCIS WADE
Translated by FREDERICK OAKELEY
Music adapted by JOHN FRANCIS WADE

VOCAL AEROBICS — WEEK 25

MON

Topic: Consonant, NG

The consonant combination *ng* is a voiced continuant sound. The tip of the tongue is forward, while the back of the tongue is raised against the soft palate. Breath is emitted through the nose. Always sing *ng* on the pitch of the vowel that precedes it; do not follow *ng* with a *hard g* sound. (For example, don't sing "song-guh.") Though there are some words—e.g., "longer"—that follow *ng* with a *hard g*, these are the exception, not the rule.

Sing_ long_ clang_ tongue_ young king spring. Song_ sung a-mong_ young_ swing-ing kings.

Sing-ing ring-ing go-ing spring-ing king-ly wing-ed sing-er.

TUE

Topics: Diatonic scale; portamento

Take moment and look closely at the music example below. It is not as complicated as it might first appear. What we have is a simple D-major scale (but you can use any major scale you choose), ascending then descending. To move from one pitch to the next let's employ a portamento, sliding between the two notes, much like a trombone player. Keep the sound smooth, even, and well-supported; breathe as indicated. Use a hum the first time, then *oo* and *ee*, as shown. The audio track should clarify any questions you might have.

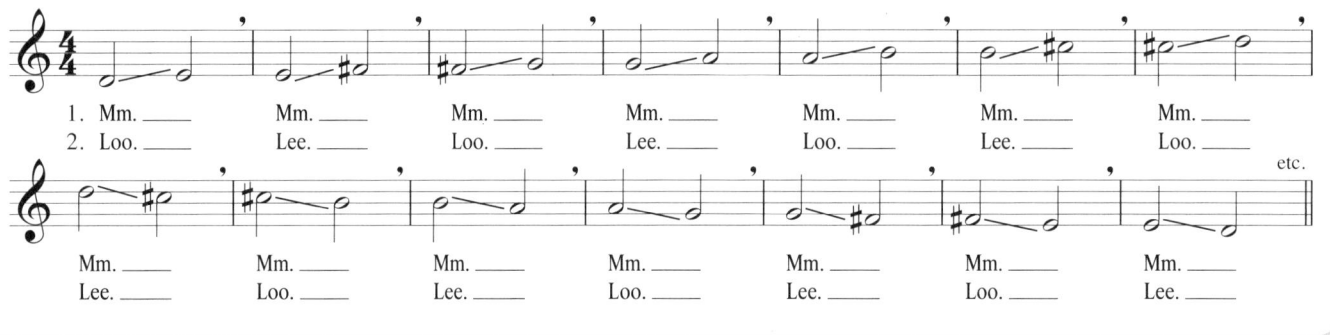

1. Mm. Mm. Mm. Mm. Mm. Mm. Mm.
2. Loo. Lee. Loo. Lee. Loo. Lee. Loo.

Mm. Mm. Mm. Mm. Mm. Mm. Mm.
Lee. Loo. Lee. Loo. Lee. Loo. Lee.

WED

Topics: Legato; phrasing; dynamics

This little D-major tune is great for practicing legato, phrasing, and dynamics. Sing on the syllables shown below. (You'll notice that they move from closed vowels to open vowels.) Keep it extra smooth and shape the melody as you go. For example, the first phrase should be a nice arc, with a crescendo as you move up the octave in bar 1, followed by a slight diminuendo in bar 2. Analyze the other phrases similarly, and pencil in expression marks and dynamics.

1. Loo. Loh.
2. Nee. Nay.

Law. Lah.
Neh. Nah.

THU — Topic: Contrast between head/chest registers

Here, we want to highlight the tonal differences between head voice and chest voice, and get a sense of the physical sensations of each. The pitches shown in the first four bars below are more advantageous for women's voices; the final four are more effective for men's voices. Women: As you sing *yah*, use the *ee-ah* tongue glide to focus the vowel. Sing legato, leaping down the octave and back up again. You can also practice this by sliding (portamento) down and back up. Men: To begin, you can employ true falsetto or a mixed registration on the top note. As you ascend by half steps for each repetition, you'll reach a point where you want an unmixed falsetto for the top note. Leap down the octave into chest voice. If it sounds like a yodel (or Carol Burnett's Tarzan yell), you're on the right track!

FRI — Topic: Singing half-steps

Singing half-steps accurately can sometimes be a challenge. Especially in the context of a descending scale pattern, the interval tends to be too wide—in other words, flat. We'll give special attention to this interval (called a minor second) from time to time. Let's use the familiar five-note major scale, and its leading tone, to highlight the half-steps that naturally occur. Sing the two-note phrases as marked. Take a little extra time on the final quarter note of each two-bar phrase and get a good breath before continuing.

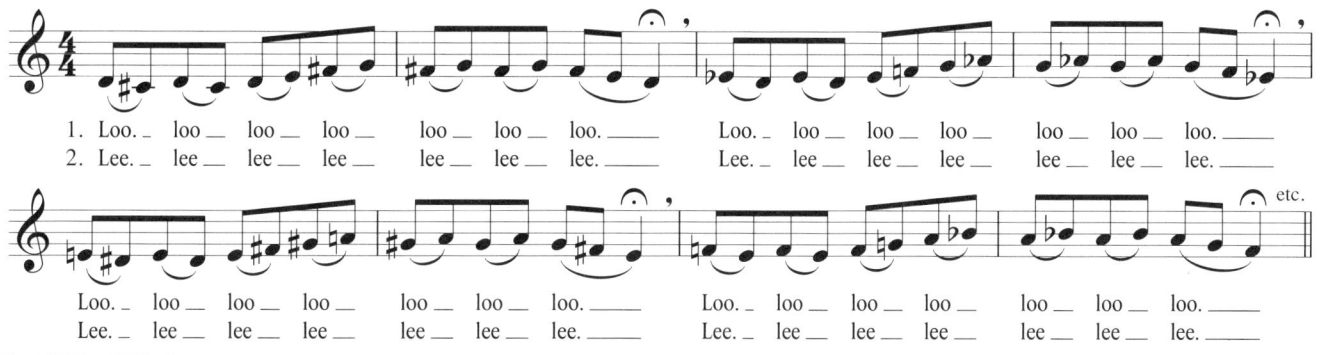

SAT — Topic: Consonants, CH & J

Say: "Charm, chill, touch." Now say: "George, joy, gem." Do you notice that *ch* and *j* (also *called soft g*) are articulated in the same manner, using the tongue and the front of the hard palate? By now, you recognize that *ch* is a voiceless sound that and *j* (soft g) is a voiced sound. Experiment, using the etude below.

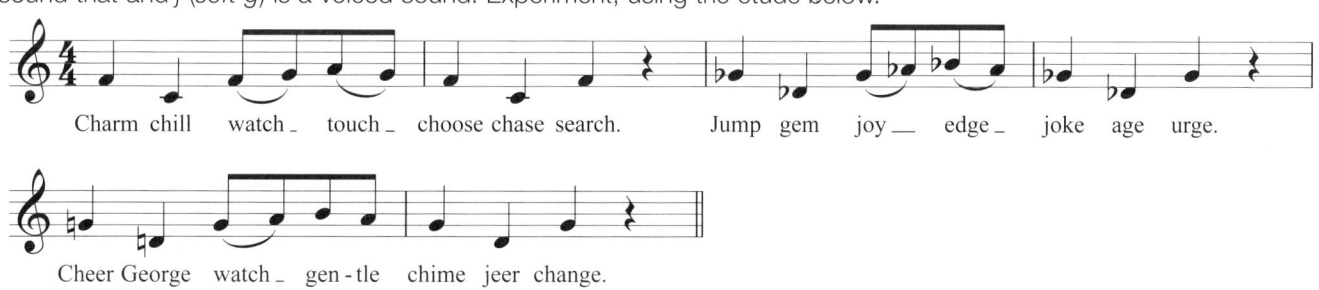

SUN — Topic: Singing expressively

The traditional English folksong "Early One Morning" spans an octave plus a fourth—not quite the vocal range required to sing "The Star-Spangled Banner," but almost! Use the transposing feature online to find the key that best suits your voice. There are several verses, but only the first is given in the music example. (You can find the whole song online or in *The Big Book of Folksongs*, HL 00312549).

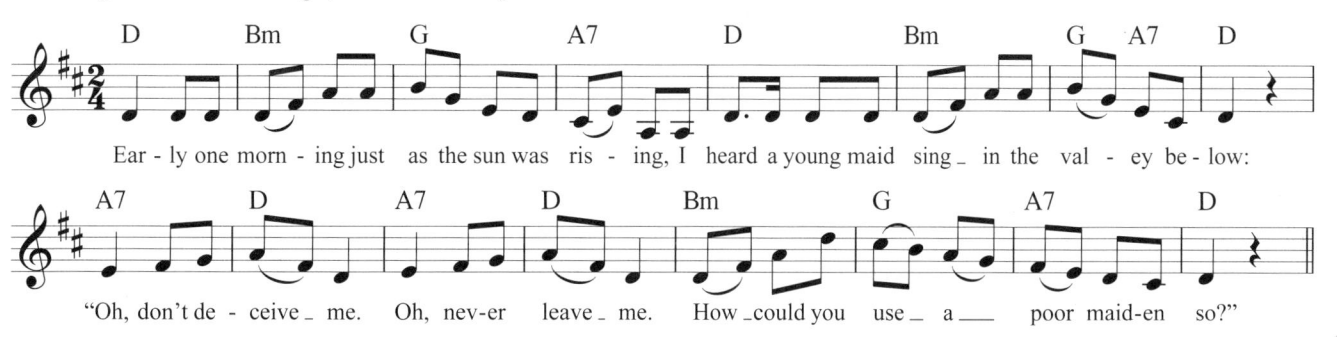

53

VOCAL AEROBICS — WEEK 26

MON
Topic: Register transition
This register transition exercise is similar to one we saw in Week 22. Again, sing at the notated pitches, starting with a sound that is predominantly chest voice. As you go higher, bring more head voice into the sound. The goal is to mix the registers, but if you need to flip entirely into head voice (falsetto), that is okay, too. If you feel any tension in your throat, stop and save this for another day. Listen to the demo before you begin.

TUE
Topics: Breathing; abdominal/back muscles; phonation; balanced onset
Today's exercise builds on a similar one in Week 1. Revisit that one before singing this one; read the text and practice singing it. The same instructions apply. Transpose the notes both up and down, across your entire range.

WED
Topics: Singing legato; expressivity
A *cantilena* is defined as "a vocal or instrumental passage of sustained lyricism." It would be hard to find a better example than the lullaby-like melody in the music example below. Taken from a piano sonata by Mozart, it's perfect for practicing legato singing. Vocalize on *loo*, giving expressive shape to the line.

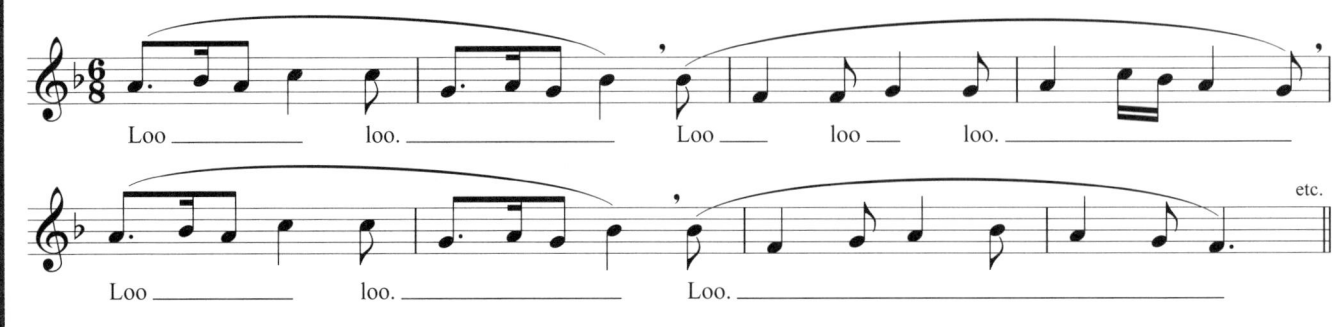

THU

Topic: Vocal strength

Take this one slowly, but not so slow that you can't sing each three-bar phrase in one breath. Remember that, in singing yah (*ee-ah*), you want to glide past *ee*—right into *ah*. Keep that vowel rich and spacious, and observe the crescendo/diminuendo indications. Notice that there are no dynamic markings; that's left for you to do.

FRI

Topic: Octaves ascending and descending

Today we're singing octaves—and sevenths, too, for that matter. Take this one slowly and allow yourself ample time to breath in bar 2. Begin with a well-shaped *ah* vowel and maintain it throughout; make sure the back of your tongue stays down and that your larynx is low and relaxed. As you make the upward leap, your air should speed up and a natural crescendo should occur. You'll need to adjust your breath pressure a bit as you descend the seventh before singing the next ascending octave. On the second half of the etude, the process is reversed: faster air on the top note, and some relaxation of breath as you sing down the octave. Listen to the demo before you begin.

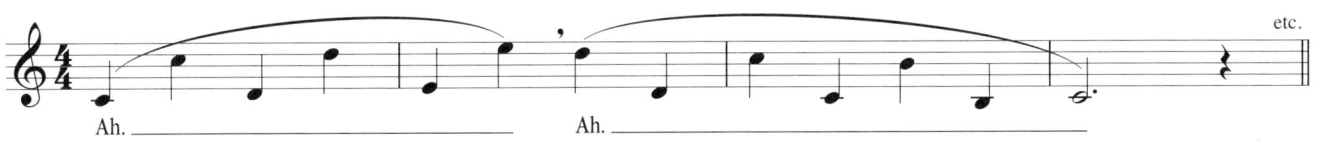

SAT

Topics: Two-note phrases; five-note scale

Today we will sing ascending thirds and descending five-note scales, inverting an aerobic we learned in Week 13. You know what to do on the two-note phrases, just be sure to begin at a tempo that will allow you to sing the 16th notes in bar 2 exactly in time. (Don't start too fast, in other words.) Notice that we're using the *ah* vowel for the scale; make certain it stays nice and open, with the soft palate raised and the back of the tongue down. Sing a few yawn-sighs before you begin.

SUN

Topics: Half steps; chromaticism; intonation

This etude is based on the opening notes of a well-known piece for solo piano. Just by looking at, can you tell which one? If not, listen to the demo track and you will recognize it immediately: Beethoven's *Für Elise*. (It's the melody that Charlie Brown's friend Schroeder loves to play!) Essentially, we have a five-note minor scale, but with a raised fourth degree in bar 1. Keep the opening half steps quite narrow. In bar 2, notice that the raised fourth degree reverts to its usual place, followed by the defining minor third. Keep your ears open. Accuracy of intonation is our chief goal here.

55

VOCAL AEROBICS — WEEK 27

MON
Topic: Triphthongs, part one

You already know that *diphthong* means "two sounds." It follows naturally, then, that *triphthong* (TRIFF-thong) means "three sounds." A triphthong is comprised of two vowel sounds, plus the neutral schwa [ə] sound. Say: "fire." Do you hear the three sounds? *Fah-ih-[ə]*. As before, the schwa replaces the *r*. Sustain the first vowel, then add the second vowel and the schwa at the very end. Listen to the demo track, then practice the exercise below.

Fire. / Fah ——— ih[ə].   Sire. / Sah ——— ih[ə].   Choir. / Kwah ——— ih[ə].   Tire. / Tah ——— ih[ə].   etc.

Briar. / Brah ——— ih[ə].   Dire. / Dah ——— ih[ə].   Liar. / Lah ——— ih[ə].   Mire. / Mah ——— ih[ə].

TUE
Topics: Strengthening the upper voice; facility; breath management

You'll notice that the first two quarter notes have both a staccato and a tenuto above them. We call this combination *portato*. Listen to the demo track and you'll hear that there the attack is that of a lengthened staccato. Pulse your diaphragm on each *mah*, then sing legato on the 16th notes (*meh*). It's a great exercise for strengthening your breathing apparatus and your upper range. Moving by half steps, take it to the top of your voice, breathing as indicated.

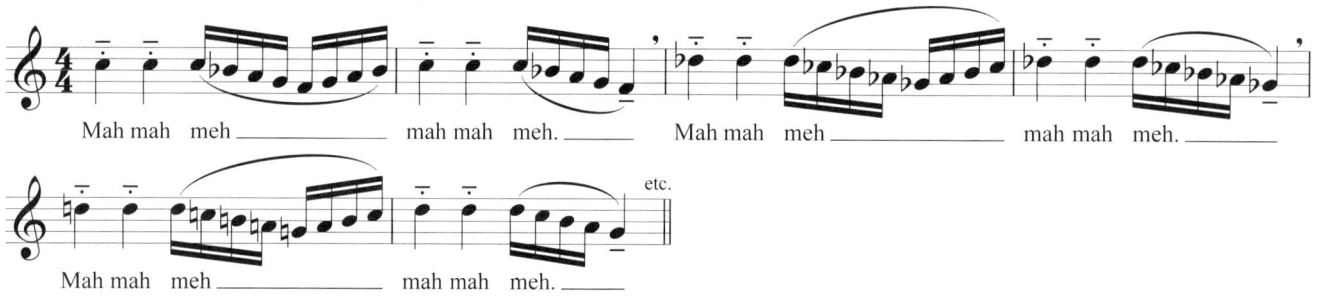

Mah mah meh ——— mah mah meh. ——— Mah mah meh ——— mah mah meh. ———

Mah mah meh ——— mah mah meh.   etc.

WED
Topic: Consonants, W & WH

W and *wh* are lip consonants. Singing *w* is actually sounding *oo* plus the vowel that follows. For example, wise = *oo-ise*, weep = *oo-eep*, and so forth. The *oo* is sung on the same pitch as the vowel that follows it, so avoid scooping into this sound. *Wh* is a voiceless sound that corresponds to the voiced *w* and might be better spelled as *hw*. Instead of singing *oo*, blow air out; when = *hwen*, what = *hwat*, etc. Notice that the exercise uses the minor mode.

Weep wail woe wise wear-y wait-ing watch.   Whip when what where why — wheth-er which.

Web while wick whence weave — whim-per work.

Topic: Tongue twister

Tongue twisters are fun! Before singing, try just speaking: "Big black rubber baby buggy bumpers." What is it about the repeated *b* that is so funny? Once you've stopped laughing, look at the indicated rhythm below; it's probably much like the way you naturally spoke the words. Do so again, tapping the quarter-note beat. Now choose a pitch and sing; move up by half steps as you go.

Topic: Major sixth vs. minor sixth; range extension

This aerobic focuses on several matters; among others: range extension, the major sixth versus the minor sixth, and moving across the vowel spectrum from closed sounds to open sounds. In bar 1, sing a major triad plus a whole step. In bar 2, sing a major triad plus a half step. Do you hear the difference between the major sixth and minor sixth? For each iteration, continue moving upward by half steps to your highest comfortable note. (Men, continue into falsetto.)

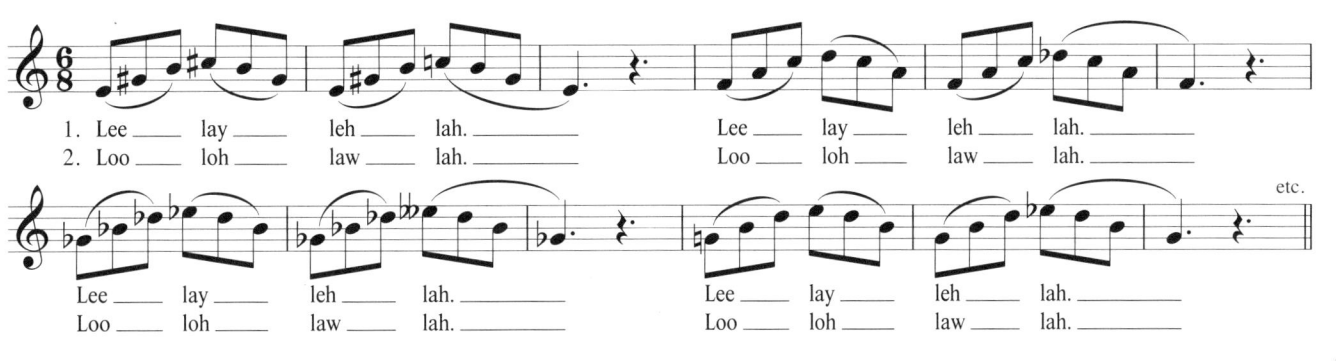

Topic: Five-note minor scale, ascending

For the most part, we've used major-scale patterns. Let's sing a minor-scale pattern. In a five-note scale, the only difference is that the third note (mi) has been lowered a half step. Sing up the scale, then rock back and forth on degrees four (fa) and five (sol). Sing the syllables indicated, moving from the closed *ee* vowel to the more open *oh* vowel. Listen to the demo track first.

Topic: Register transition exercise

Making a smooth transition from chest voice to head voice—or vice versa—is one of the challenges in building a strong voice and increasing its range. This exercise takes you from chest voice to head voice. Sing with a soft but well-supported tone in chest voice, mixing in head voice as the pitches become progressively higher. Eventually, you should be in pure head voice (falsetto). Listen to the demo before you begin.

57

WEEK 28

VOCAL AEROBICS

MON
Topics: Major scale; 3/4 time

Earlier, we sang a descending major scale in 3/4 time. (See page 29.) Today, we'll sing up the scale and back down again, mixing it up with various vowel sounds. Start slowly at first, increasing the tempo as you become more adept. As you sing, take note of the way you're shaping the vowels—and always make sure the leading tone (ti-do, do-ti) is in tune.

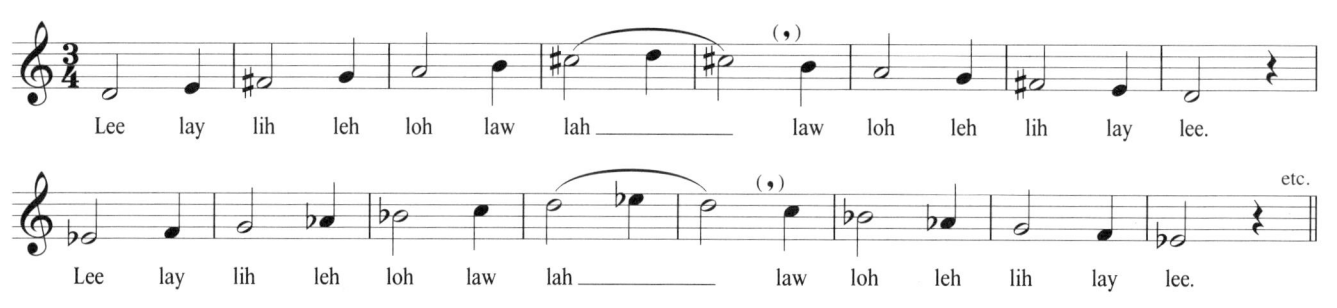

TUE
Topics: Vowel focus; strengthening the voice.

Today we elaborate on an aerobic from Week 14. First, spend a few minutes practicing that one. The accented *hing* shown below should bring your sound immediately into focus. Continue the *ng* as you open into the vowel that follows. Sing a well-supported *forte* and be accurate with the rhythm. Inhale at the indicated breath marks.

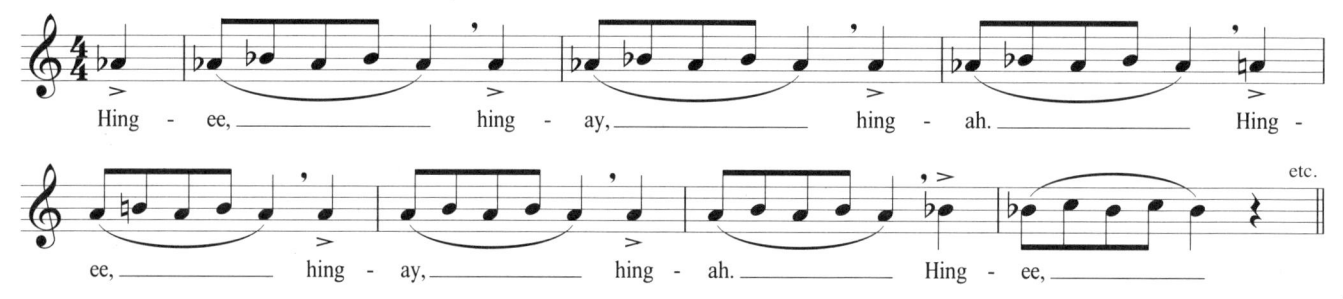

WED
Topic: Singing fourths and fifths

Here's another etude to challenge your ears. This time, we're moving up the scale singing ascending fifths and descending fourths. Coming back down we reverse the order, intoning descending fifths and ascending fourths. Use a staccato articulation and aim for the center of the pitch. This can be a bit tricky, so sit at the piano if need be.

Topics: Sequences; breath; flexibility

Look closely at the music example below. You'll notice that, from the tonic (root note), there is an upward leap of a sixth. What follows is the same melodic pattern stated three times, but at different pitch levels. This is called a "sequence," a common compositional technique. This four-bar phrase, based on a similar one by J.S. Bach, wends its way downward to conclude on the tonic. Work to sing it in a single breath, concentrating on pitch accuracy, flexibility, and breath management. Keep it smooth, avoiding any "bumps" in your sound.

Topics: Opening up the voice; singing forte

Yah! (Or "ja," as German speakers would say.) This etude can really help open up your voice to a full, rich tone quality. We're singing a descending major-chord arpeggio, moving by half steps for each repetition. Use a well-supported forte for this one. The sound's natural tendency will be a diminuendo, but offset that by keeping your fast air moving through that final dotted-half note. Think *ee-ah*, allowing the *ee* to focus that open *ah* vowel for you. Use only your tongue for the *ee* to *ah* transition. No chin movement—and no gum chewing—allowed for this one.

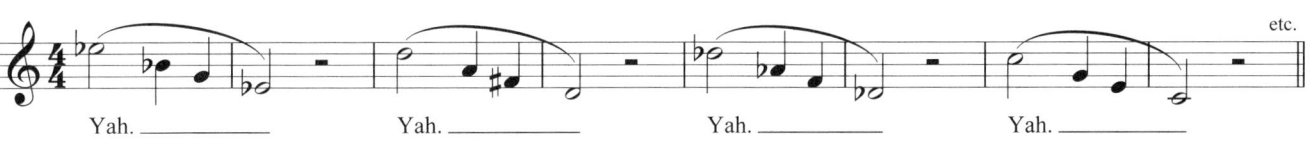

Topic: Using your imagination for syllables, articulation, dynamics, etc.

We're leaving you to your own devices for this simple, folksong-like tune in E major. Use your imagination for syllables, articulation, dynamics, etc. Here are just a few suggestions to get you started: 1) sing each note staccato on *bim* or *doo*; 2) sing molto legato on *loh*; 3) experiment with dynamics, crescendo, diminuendo, etc.

Topics: Minor key; compound meter; two-bar phrases

At first glance, you might think this etude is in F major, because of the B-flat in the key signature. Upon closer inspection, and after singing it, you'll realize it is in the relative key of D minor. (Notice that the first and last notes are both Ds.) Sing each two-bar phrase in a single breath, experimenting with various tempos. How does the character of the music change, based on its speed?

59

VOCAL AEROBICS — WEEK 29

MON
Topics: Five-note minor scale, descending, with leading tone
In Week 27, we sang an ascending five-note minor scale. Let's reverse that and sing downward, adding the leading tone (ti) at the end. Where are the half steps? Circle them in your music, and be sure to keep the interval narrow. It's all too easy to go flat on those notes, especially when descending.

TUE
Topics: Focusing the voice; strengthening the chest voice
This goo-goo-goofy etude will serve to strengthen the middle and lower parts of your voice. Recall that we refer to *g* as a hard, voiced consonant; it allows a strong start into each phrase. Ensure that its pitch is the same as the *oo*; no scooping allowed! Begin mezzo forte and crescendo across the triplets and the half note. As you descend the major arpeggio, keep the sound full. The *g* will help assure a solid attack on each note. Move down by half step until you have reached your lowest comfortable note.

WED
Topics: Chromaticism; half steps and whole steps across a perfect fourth.
Today, let's give our ears a robust workout, singing half steps and whole steps across an ascending perfect fourth. To help you along, the half steps are marked with a carat, and the whole steps are marked with a bracket. Bar 2 leaps down to the starting note, then back up. This one is a bit tricky, so you might want to listen to the demo track first.

THU

Topic: Women, chest voice and head voice

Ladies, here's one for you! In bar 1, sing the bottom notes in your chest voice, staccato. Use a full sound. Leap up the octave and sing those notes in head voice. Keep it strong and use the diaphragmatic muscles for a good *staccato* articulation. In bar 2, sing legato, up and over. Move up by half steps, taking the chest voice as high as you comfortably can. Stop if you feel any throat tension whatsoever.

FRI

Topics: Minor triads; range extension

We're working to keep the "minor" sound in our ears and brains—singing a minor chord arpeggio, then leaping from "do" to "fa" to "sol" and back down, then intoning a descending five-note minor scale. Take it slowly at first, ensuring that your pitches are right on the money. This is also a good range extension exercise, so take it as high as you comfortably can.

SAT

Topic: Upward range extension

Let's return to a familiar pattern—the octave arpeggio—to create an etude for upward range extension. When you reach the top of the pattern in bar 2, bounce back to *sol* a couple of times; at that moment, tilt your head back a bit to make sure your neck muscles don't "grab." Though the time signatures change, the quarter-note pulse is consistent.

SUN

Topic: Tongue twister

In a previous tongue twister, a recurring *b* consonant provided the challenge. Here, it's the *l* and the *th* sounds, both of which are voiced consonant. As before, start by speaking the words slowly, then adding the notated rhythm, then singing on a chosen pitch.

VOCAL AEROBICS — WEEK 30

MON

Topics: Octave scale ascending; articulations

Before you sing today's exercise, review the one from Tuesday in Week 21. This is the same octave pattern, but inverted. It's natural to have a built-in crescendo as you ascend. Let that happen, and keep the final quarter note strong and well-supported.

TUE

Topic: Pitch accuracy

Today's etude is good for your ear as well as your voice. We're covering an octave, but singing only the root, fifth, and root (an octave higher), using the *solfege* syllables *do* and *sol*. (Remember the song "Do-Re-Mi" from *The Sound of Music*?) Take this one slowly, giving full value to each note. Keep the sound full and supported. Breathe on the quarter rests and move accurately to the next pitch.

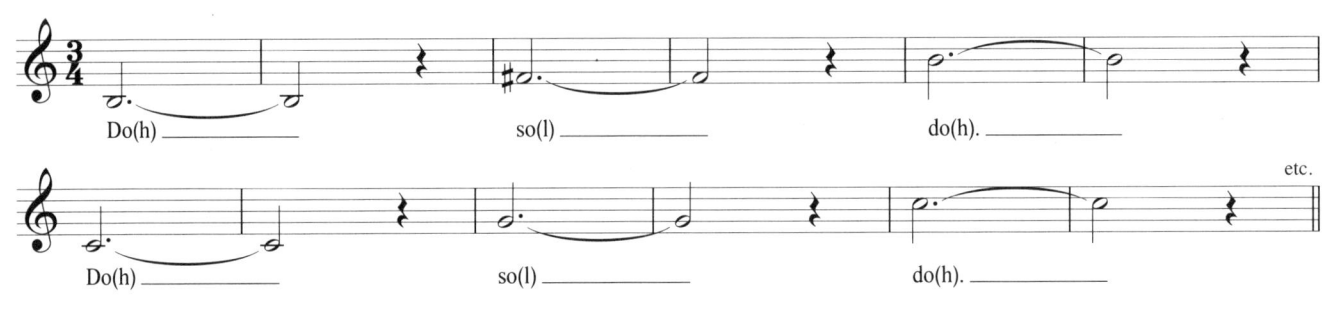

WED

Topic: Preliminary chromatic scale exercise

When singing our favorite songs, rarely are we called up to execute an extensive chromatic scale. However, for ear-training and pitch acuity, it's a valuable skill to have in our toolbox. Here's an exercise that builds on the one in Week 10. Sing up the five-note major scale. As you come back down, add both the lowered third (*me*) and the lowered second (*ra*).

THU

Topics: Range extension; flexibility

Whether we're riffing on the latest pop hit or singing an 18th-century aria, it's important to be able to move our voices flexibly. This etude will help. It elaborates on a descending five-note scale, singing the scale and its neighbor notes in a triplet rhythm. As you can see in the printed example, there are three notes within each quarter-note beat. At the bottom of the scale we come to rest on a dotted-half note. Ultimately, we want to sing each two-bar phrase on a single legato vowel, but in the early stages you might try singing a staccato syllable (like *bim*) on each note. Play the five-note scale on your keyboard and sing the curlicues around it. Listen to the demo track before you start.

FRI

Topic: Alternating major/minor triad arpeggios

In Weeks 14 and 17, we sang major and minor octave arpeggios. Today, we mix it up and alternate those. The same instructions apply. Refer to pages 30 and 36 before you begin, and sing syllables of your choosing.

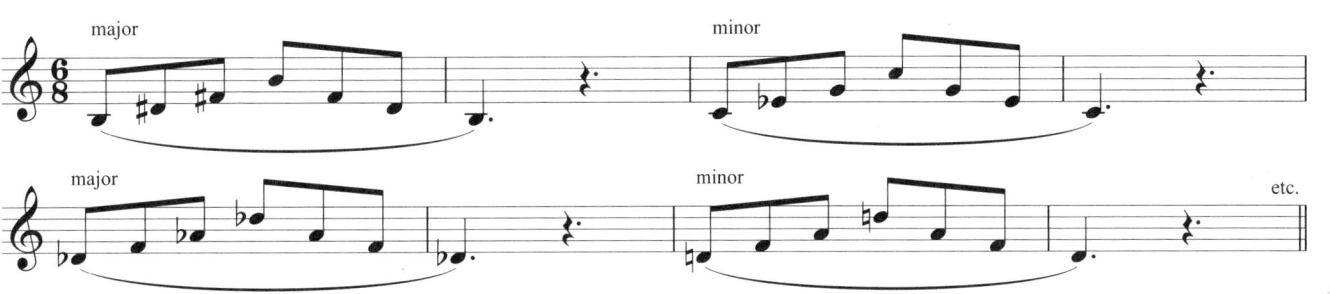

SAT

Topic: Triphthongs, part two

Think of this as Triphthongs, Part 2. Say: "our flower power." Each of those words uses the triphthong *ah-oo-[ə]*. Notice that the sound can be spelled *-our* or *-ower*; they sound exactly alike. For example: flour, flower. Listen to the online audio, then sing the etude. The *oo* and schwa [ə] come after the long-held *ah*.

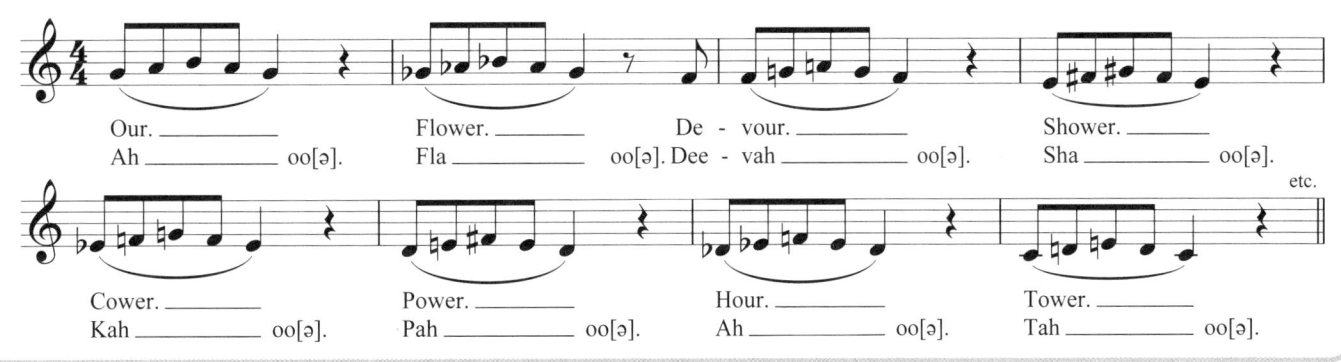

SUN

Topics: Ties; phrase shape; syncopation

Here are a couple of phrases from a Neapolitan folksong called "The Fair Maid of Sorrento"—or "La vera Sorrentina" if you prefer its Italian title. Use a slight crescendo on the tied notes, to give an express little nudge into the next part of the phrase. Sing on *lah*, using a bright Italianate sound—just like Pavarotti would! (Did you notice the use of melodic sequence, as we saw in Week 28?)

VOCAL AEROBICS

WEEK 31

MON

Topics: Dynamics; breath management

Begin with a firm forte and re-engage your breathing muscles on each eighth rest, observing the diminuendo as you descend. Use your fast air on the way back up and conclude with the same strong sound with which you began.

TUE

Topics: Range extension; staccato

This fun exercise is great for extending the top of your range, allowing you to sing even higher. It is an octave arpeggio, sung staccato; give the final quarter note its full value and breathe on the quarter rest. When you've reached your topmost comfortable note, stop. If you feel your throat starting to tighten, stop. If you feel any muscle tension in your neck, stop. Progress takes time and patience, so keep it healthy. We've indicated the syllable *hah*, but add others of your choosing as well.

WED

Topics: Flexibility; even sound

This etude, a descending octave in triplets, offers all sorts of possibilities—and is good for your ear as well as your voice. First sing on a hum, then with various syllables, then with a single legato vowel. Singing the entire phrase in a single breath is the goal, but work slowly at first to ensure pitch accuracy. As always, listen for the half steps between ti-do and mi-fa to be well-tuned.

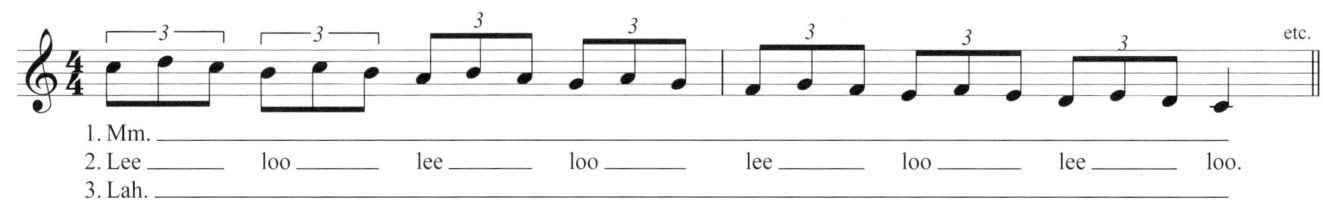

THU

Topics: Musicality; phrase shape

Let's use this phrase to practice phrasing and musicality. It's taken from "Nymphs and Shepherds," a song by the late 17th-century composer Henry Purcell. (Do a web search for the printed music and a full performance.) First sing on a hum, then with syllables, then with the antiquated text.

FRI

Topic: Tongue-twister

Here's a tongue-twister we all know: "Peter Piper picked a peck of pickled peppers." We've set it to a five-note major scale and added some amusing rhythms. Start slowly enough that you can articulate the 16th notes distinctly. Increase the tempo as you become more adept. Have fun!

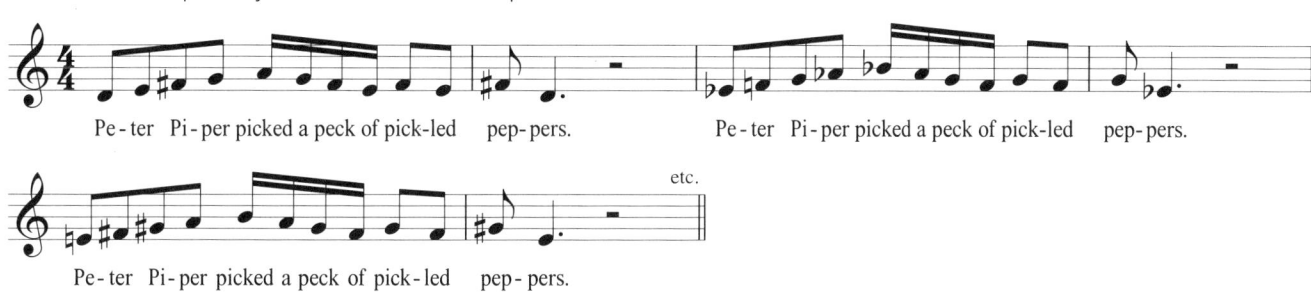

SAT

Topic: Perfect fourth vs. augmented fourth

The pattern in the first two bars should look familiar: It's the five-note major scale. Bar 3 is the same, except that the fourth scale degree has been raised a half-step, creating the interval of an augmented fourth between that note and the starting pitch. Listen to the demo and you'll hear the difference. The raised fourth acts as a sort of leading tone to the fifth (*sol*)—as in the first two notes of the song "Maria," from Leonard Bernstein's epic musical, *West Side Story*. (Find an online performance.) Descend via a major triad arpeggio.

SUN

Topics: Passagio for men

Here's a melodic pattern—a triad arpeggio plus the sixth note (*la*) of the scale—you can sing in any part of your voice range, using a lip trill, a hum, or whatever vowels you choose. The exercise shown below, however, is specially designed to help you gents move up into the *passagio*—the Italian word for "passage"—that part of the voice between the two registers. Use a lip trill as you ascend, then an *ee* vowel on the way down. Your target note is the same one you started on, not the highest.

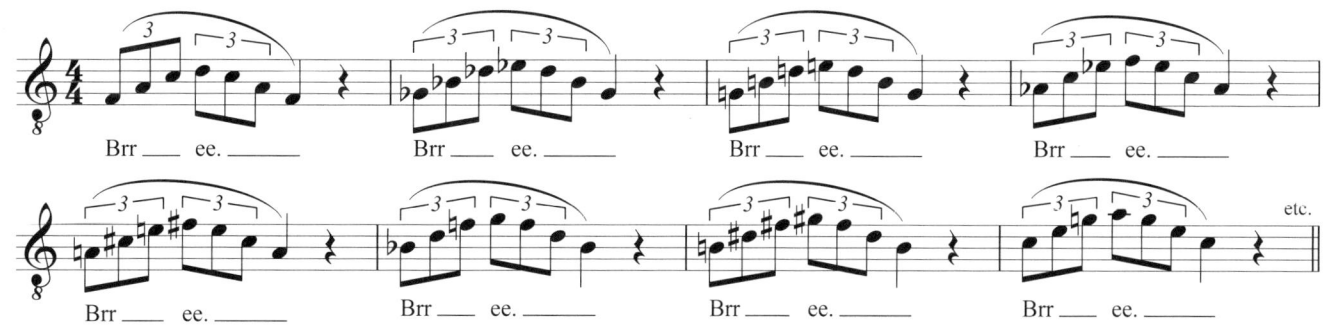

65

VOCAL AEROBICS — WEEK 32

"The Jolly Miller" is a jovial British folksong that dates back at least to the 18th century. (You'll sometimes hear it called "The Miller of Dee.") The River Dee is located in the United Kingdom, and flows 68 miles through both England and Wales. In an earlier age, it was host to any number of water-powered mill wheels that turned huge stones to grind grain into meal and flour.

The song tells the story of a happy-go-lucky—if somewhat cynical—miller who doesn't mind hard work, but also enjoys his pint of ale at the local pub. Take a look at the lead sheet on page 67 and you'll see that, following a four-bar introduction, the music falls easily into four-bar phrases. The first and second phrases are identical, the third phrase (the bridge; see page 18) is entirely different, and the final phrase is a modified version of the first two. We could chart its form like this: A–A–B–A1; it's a formula often seen in folk music, hymns, and even in certain pop songs.

Because of the melody's repetitive nature, the notes of the song are fairly easy to learn. The fun comes in finding ways to characterize the text—through dynamics, articulation, word stress, tone colors, etc. Let's explore some of these possibilities, taking one verse at a time.

Verse 1: We set the stage by introducing the miller and describing certain aspects of his character. (The word "burden" here refers to the song's chorus, a use of the term that dates from the 17th century.) Then we hear the miller himself speak: "I care for nobody…" Commence with a light, dancelike approach, with a sparkle in your eye and in your voice. When the miller speaks, sing legato, with a richer, more self-important tone.

Verse 2: The miller is still speaking, so continue in the manner that ended verse 1. Imagine that, as the boasting miller, your chest is proudly puffed up and your thumbs are hooked behind your suspenders. Accent the notes on "push, push, push" and have fun with the *sh* sounds. The bowl mentioned here is, of course, one containing the ale. For "the longer we sit here and drink, the merrier we shall be," you might feign slight inebriation.

Verse 3: Now you, the narrator, are telling us the moral of the story: Life is short, so eat, drink, and be merry while you still can. How do you want to characterize this message? Is it merry and lighthearted? Austere and ominous? Do you want to sing it full out—or with a bit more wink-wink-nudge-nudge innuendo? These are your choices and you can change your interpretation from one performance to another.

"The Jolly Miller" is set in a rollicking 6/8 meter and cast in a minor key. One octave is the required vocal range. This brief warm-up covers all three of those aspects. Sing on the vowels indicated.

Nee.
Noh.
Nah.

The Jolly Miller

English Folksong

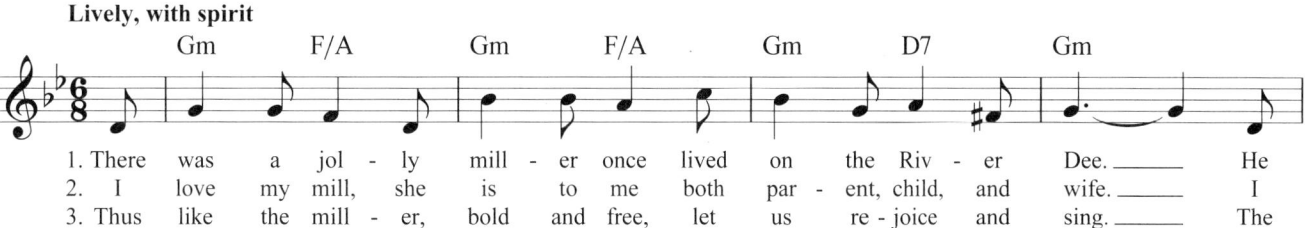

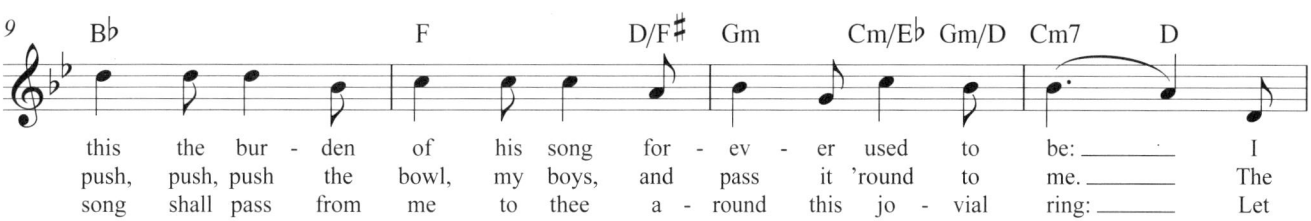
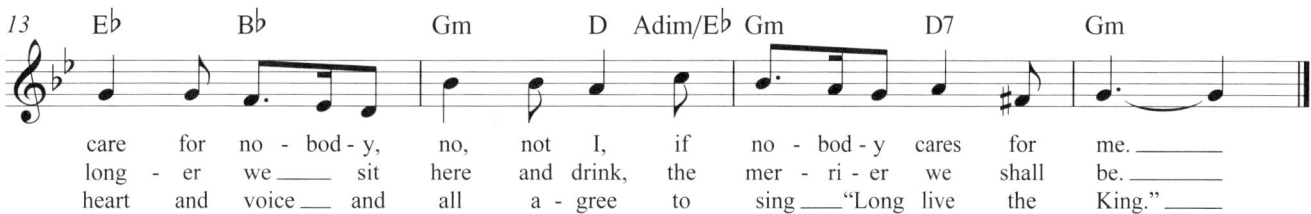

VOCAL AEROBICS
WEEK 33

MON

Topics: Flexibility; minor scale

Agility in a minor scale is our goal with this etude. Eventually, you'll want to move quickly and accurately across the three-bar pattern, singing only a single vowel sound, as shown below. To begin learning the melody, however, sing a staccato *bim* on each note. Go slowly at first; increase the tempo each day.

TUE

Topics: Portamento; chromatic scale, ascending

Today we're going to build on an exercise from Week 25. In that instance we sang a diatonic major scale, sliding from one note to the next. Here, we're going to practice an ascending chromatic scale, covering all the notes of the octave. Refer to your piano keyboard. We'll sing all the notes, both black and white, from one D up to the next D (or whatever note you choose). As before, use portamento, employ good breath support, and keep the sound smooth; observe the breath marks. Use *nn* the first time, then mix it up with vowel sounds.

WED

Topic: Chromatic scale, from tonic up to four

You're getting so good at chromatic scales that it's time to add another one! We're moving from the tonic (*do*) up to the fourth (*fa*) and back down via half steps. Look at the music example below. Notice that we have used enharmonic spellings; for example, F♯ = G♭; G♯ = A♭, etc. This is in keeping with standard music notation, in which sharps are used when ascending and flats are used when descending. Naturals are used as needed.

THU

Topic: Chromatic scale, from tonic down to five

Following up on yesterday's aerobic, let's sing chromatically from the tonic (*do*) down to the fifth (*sol*) and back up again. You may want to use a keyboard when first practicing these half-step exercises. Ultimately, though, strive to sing them accurately on your own. Make sure that your breath is moving freely and that your throat is relaxed. Use that big muscle in your cranium, not the ones in your neck.

FRI

Topics: Flexibility; phrase shapes; vowels

Have fun with this one. Hum. Sing on staccato syllables. Sing on various vowels, both open and closed. Sing the whole five bars in one breath on a single syllable. Experiment with articulations. Use your imagination. Like an etude in Week 31, the melody comes from Purcell's "Nymphs and Shepherds." Look it up!

SAT

Topics: Five-note scale; half-step; leading tone

Here's the five-note scale, but with a couple of twists and turns on the way down. It's actually easier than it looks, so listen to the demo first. Bar 2 contains two half steps, and we'll want to tune those carefully. On beat 2 of bar 2, there's a downward leap of a tritone, a tricky interval to sing. If you think of the bottom note as the leading tone back to the tonic (*do*), it'll be easier to incite. The indicated syllables move from a closed *oo* to an open *ah*, sung legato. Mix it up by singing a staccato *doot* on each note.

SUN

Topic: Octave chromatic scale, quarter notes

As we have learned this week, the chromatic scale is based on an octave of 12 half-steps, as opposed to the seven-note diatonic scale. The music example below shows a chromatic scale ascending from middle C up to the next C, then coming back down again. (In truth, you can start on any note to sing this scale.) At first, you'll want to use your keyboard to ensure accuracy; eventually, you'll be able to sing it unaided. Use the initial *t* sound to help focus the vowel and center the pitch.

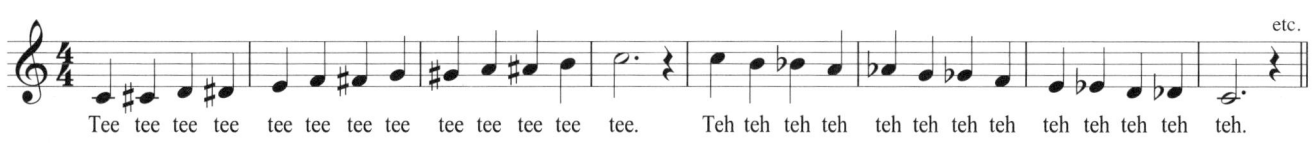

VOCAL AEROBICS — WEEK 34

MON
Topics: Breath support; flexibility; warming up

Today's exercise is the inversion of one we practiced in Week 10. Review it before tackling this aerobic. Sing forte with good abdominal and back support. Keep the tone full and vibrant as you descend the five-note scale and come back up again. Allow the initial *h* to get your breath started. This is a good warm-up to include in your daily practice.

Heh. Hah.

TUE
Topics: Skipping; note accuracy

This etude is a lot of fun! Study the printed example for a moment. What do you notice? That's correct; it's a simple octave scale, ascending then descending, with upper (ascending) and lower (descending) neighbor notes thrown in. In each instance, the interval of a third is followed by the interval of a second. Crescendo as you go up, diminuendo as you come down, always aiming to sing each note dead-center. What syllables should you sing? We're leaving that up to you. Perhaps begin by singing *dee* or *bim* on each eighth note. Once you can sing accurately, try intoning a single vowel sound for each two-bar phrase. Listen to the demo track for a couple of examples.

WED
Topics: Range extension; vocal strength; pitch accuracy

From the first note of the scale (*do*), we leap up to the fifth note (*sol*), then to the octave (*do*) and back, then descend stepwise. (*sol-fa-mi-re-do*). If it helps you, sing first on the solfege syllables. (Make Maria von Trapp happy!) Keep *yah* (*ee-ah*) full and strong, avoiding a diminuendo on the way back down. This etude will help strengthen your voice, so sing it throughout your comfortable range.

Yah yah yah yah yah. Yah yah yah yah yah.

Yah yah yah yah yah. Yah yah yah yah yah.

THU

Topic: Octave scale, incrementally

Look closely at the aerobic below. Do you notice that we are singing a descending octave scale, but incrementally? Our ultimate goal is to sing each big four-bar phrase in a single breath on a single vowel. If need be, though, break it down into smaller segments and sing syllables on each note. That's the way we learn songs, so it makes sense to do the same here.

FRI

Topic: Tongue twister; arpeggios

"If a dog chews shoes, whose shoes does he choose?" You can consider that a rhetorical question or—if you have a shoe-chewing dog—actually answer it. In either case, we're singing major chord arpeggios, moving by half steps at each new measure. Practice two ways: 1) one-measure phrases; 2) two-measure phrases. Is one way easier than the other? Why? (There's no right answer to *that* question.)

SAT

Topic: Syncopation

This syncopated aerobic has a folk-like, south-of-the-border feel. Use a well-articulated *t* to point up the rhythm. (Review the lesson on *t* in Week 13.) Listen to the demo, then use the online backing track to sing this toe-tapper in several keys. Clap on beats 2 and 4.

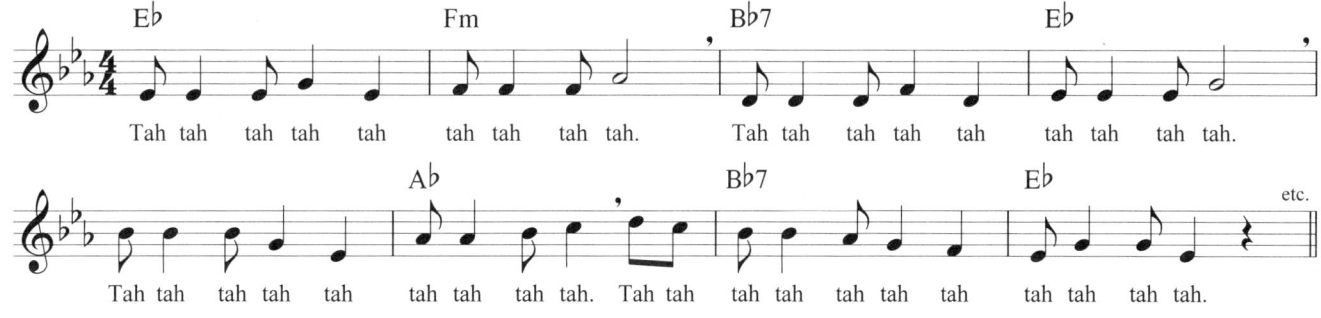

SUN

Topic: Syncopated song

Let's sing a melody that uses the off-beat rhythm we practiced yesterday. "Somebody's Knocking at Your Door" is a traditional African-American spiritual. You can highlight its energetic syncopation by accenting the quarter notes as indicated. In addition to the demo, there's a piano-only track.

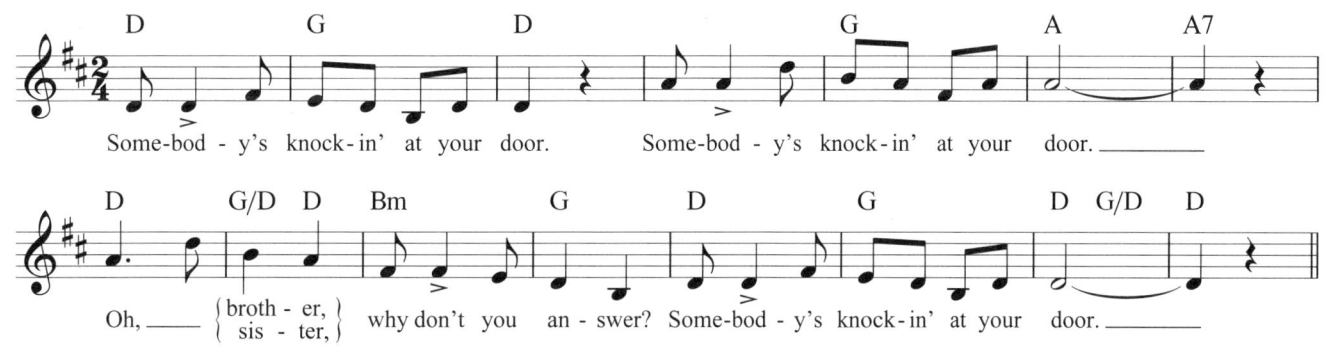

VOCAL AEROBICS — WEEK 35

MON
Topics: Portamento; chromatic scale, descending

Let's reverse the vocalise we sang in Week 33. There, we sang an ascending chromatic, employing portamento. Here, we're going to descend by half steps. (Remember: The piano keyboard can be your best friend.) Sing all the notes, both black and white, from one D down to the next D (or whatever note you choose). As before, slide smoothly, use good support, and pay attention to the breath marks. Use a hum the first time, then try it with various vowel sounds.

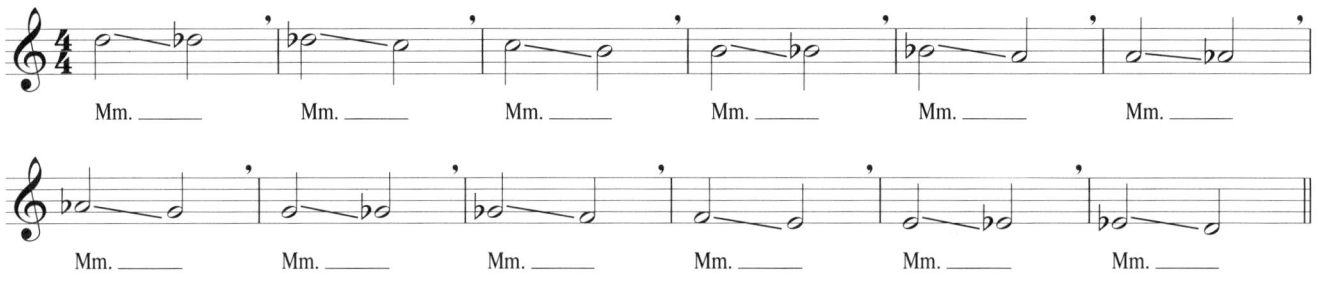

TUE
Topic: Flexibility

If you've sung in a choir—or gone shopping in December—you may recognize this snippet from the Christmas portion of Handel's *Messiah*. It is taken from the chorus "For Unto Us a Child Is Born," and requires solid support, good breath management, and vocal flexibility. Keep it light and bouncy and give a slight emphasis to each beat, first practicing on syllables as in Week 22. Notice that Handel uses the sequencing technique we saw in Week 28.

WED
Topics: Intonation; articulation

As we've seen before, it's fun to use a well-known tune as a vocalise. "In the Hall of the Mountain King" is a minor-key melody by the 19th-century Norwegian composer Edvard Grieg, written as incidental music for Ibsen's play *Peer Gynt*. Sing each note on *doo*, observing the staccato and tenuto markings. We're aiming to be absolutely spot-on for every pitch. Watch out for the accidentals in bars 2 and 6. (Tip: From F♯ to E♯ is a half-step.)

THU
Topics: Repeated notes; two-note phrases; expressivity; upward leaps

We've practiced two-note phrases in several exercises. Let's use that concept to sing repeated notes across two-bar phrases. Give special attention to the vowel shapes and keep the sound smooth and well-supported. Enjoy the expressive upward leaps of a major sixth in bars 3 and 5. First, listen to the demo, then sing along with the backing track. Use the transposing feature to sing the melody in several keys.

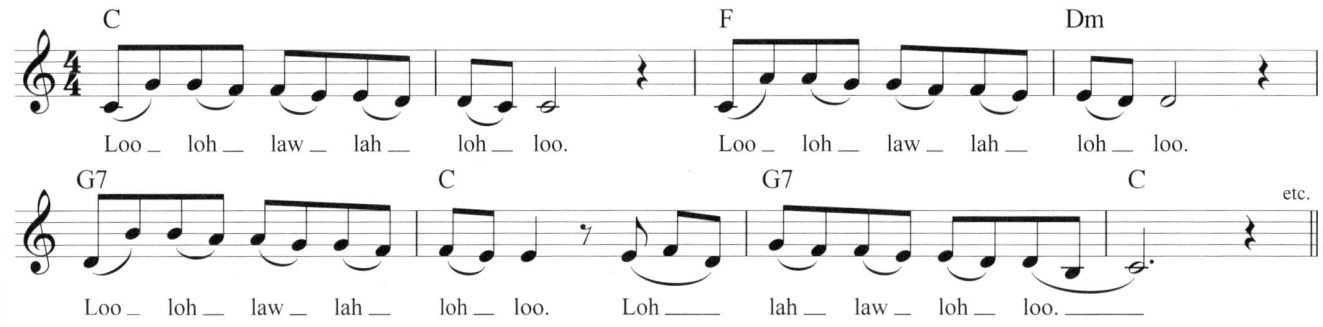

FRI

Topics: Flexibility; register transition, head to chest

This aerobic allows us to kill the proverbial two birds with one stone: we can work on both flexibility and transitioning from head voice into chest voice. Take a look at the music example. You'll see that we're in compound meter, descending an octave, with fancy neighboring tones thrown in. Our goal is to sing smoothly and evenly across the four-bar phrase; there should be no bumps. Sing at the notated pitch, moving down by half steps after every phrase. Eventually, you'll start mixing in chest voice. Let the breath work for you; there should be no tension in your throat.

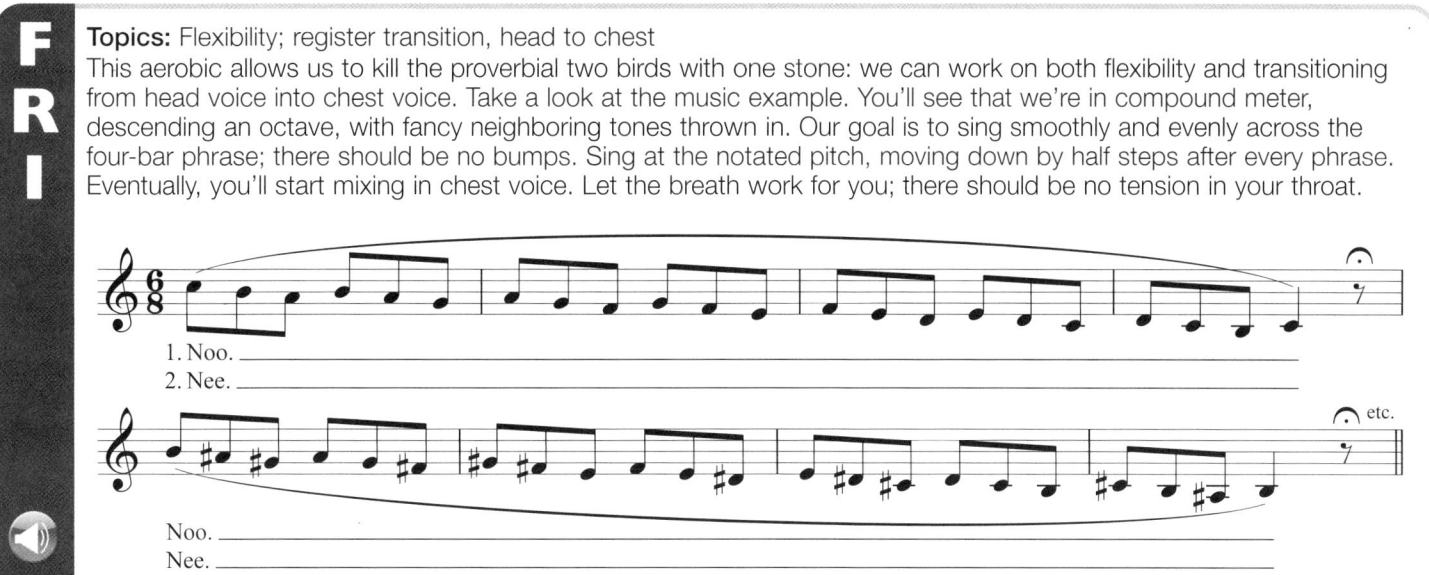

SAT

Topics: Syncopation; across-the-bar syncopation

Look at this etude in 2/4 time. It's chock-full of syncopation, both within the bar and across the bar lines. Before singing or listening to the demo, practice speaking the rhythm on *bim*. Include the accents as indicated. Did you notice, beginning in the second big phrase (bar 4), that there is a string of off-the-beat quarter notes? This sort of rhythm is often found in jazz. Isn't it fun?

SUN

Topic: Rhythmic acuity; pitch accuracy

As we've seen earlier it's sometimes fun to fashion the melody of a song into a vocalise. This one has a few curve balls, and will test your rhythmic and pitch acuity. There are some fast-moving 16th notes and a few accidentals, so start by practicing it slowly. Eventually, though, it should be fast and jaunty. It's folksong from Poland called "Krakowiak." You needn't be proficient in Polish, because we're going to sing it on syllables. There's even a piano-only track!

73

VOCAL AEROBICS — WEEK 36

MON
Topics: Natural minor scale; range extension; agility; ö umlaut

We haven't sung the *ö* umlaut in quite a while. (Review Thursday of Week 5 if you need a quick reminder.) You'll notice we're using a natural minor scale, working our way up the octave, then coming straight back down. Allow the umlaut to focus your sound; alternate *ö* with *oh*, as shown. The tempo should be rather fast, but you may want to start slowly at first, and work in smaller melodic fragments. Employ the practice tools you've learned—and listen to the demo.

TUE
Topics: Vocal strength; dynamics; crescendo/diminuendo; balanced onset

Take a look at the exercise below and you'll see that a good deal of information is given there. In addition to the usual notes, rhythms, and syllables, there are dynamic markings, slurs, accents, and crescendo/diminuendo indications. This may seem like a lot to take in, so study the example for a bit. It's a good aerobic for strengthening your voice, among other things.

The first bar allows you to practice a balanced onset; keep it moderately soft. In the second bar, sing the "hairpins" as indicated; keep it smooth. Finally, crescendo the dotted-half-note in bar 3. If you like, replenish your breath after each quarter in bar 1; otherwise, be sure to catch a breath before bar 2.

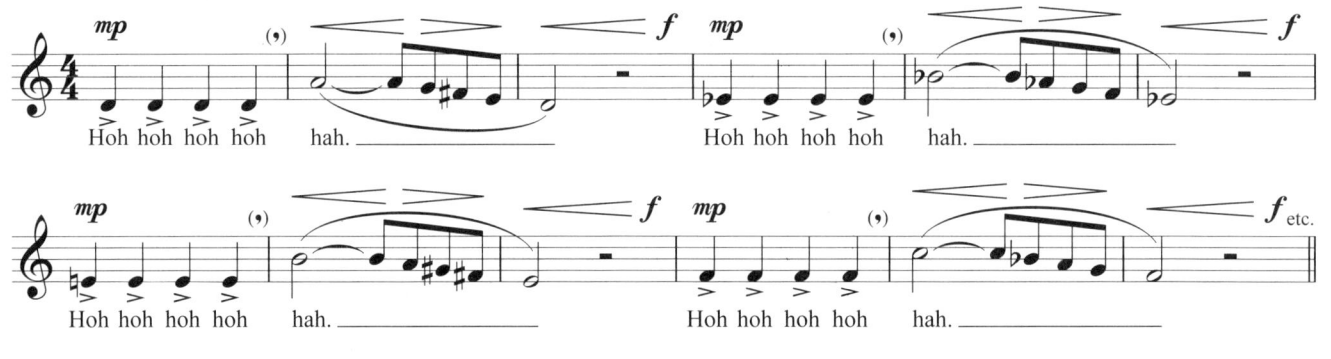

WED
Topics: Flexibility; range; minor pattern; vowels, closed to open

This minor-key melody will allow you to increase your vocal agility, hone your vowel shapes, extend your range, and test your pitch accuracy. Eventually, the tempo should be quite fast, with each two-bar iteration sung in a single breath. Start slowly, increasing the speed as you become comfortable with the notes. The vowels move from closed to open: *mee-may-mah*.

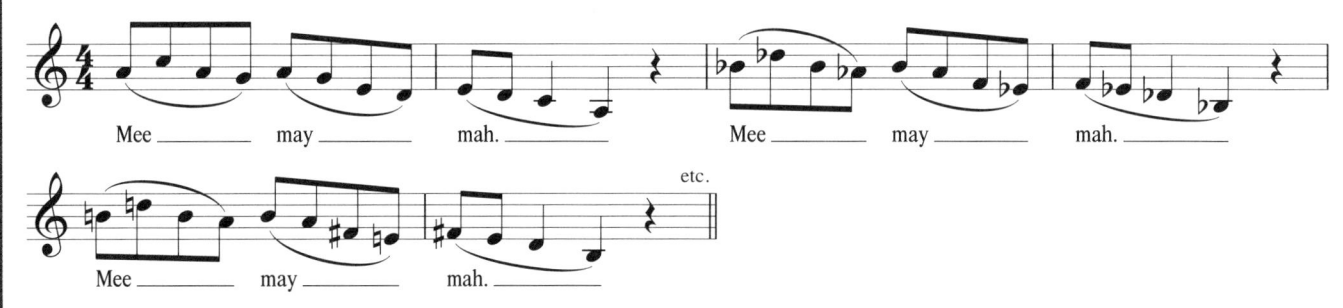

THU

Topics: Augmentation; flexibility; vowels

In today's aerobic, the note values begin to double: from 16ths to eighths; from eighths to quarter; from quarter to half. The fancy term for this is *augmentation*. This etude encourages vocal facility, rhythmic accuracy, and well-placed vowels that move from closed to open. Sing it across your entire range.

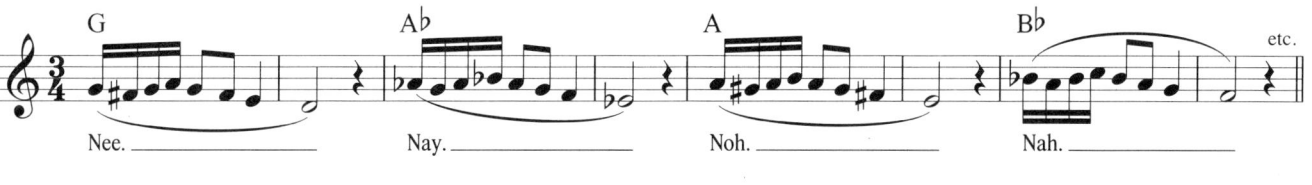

FRI

Topics: Nine-note scale; vowels, closed to open; vocal strength and agility

Today, let's turn our attention to range extension and vocal strength and agility. Begin by practicing this nine-note scale slowing and deliberately, ideally in a single breath. Crescendo as you ascend, and keep the tone strong while you switch to open vowels and descend. Over time, increase the tempo. Sing it throughout your comfortable range.

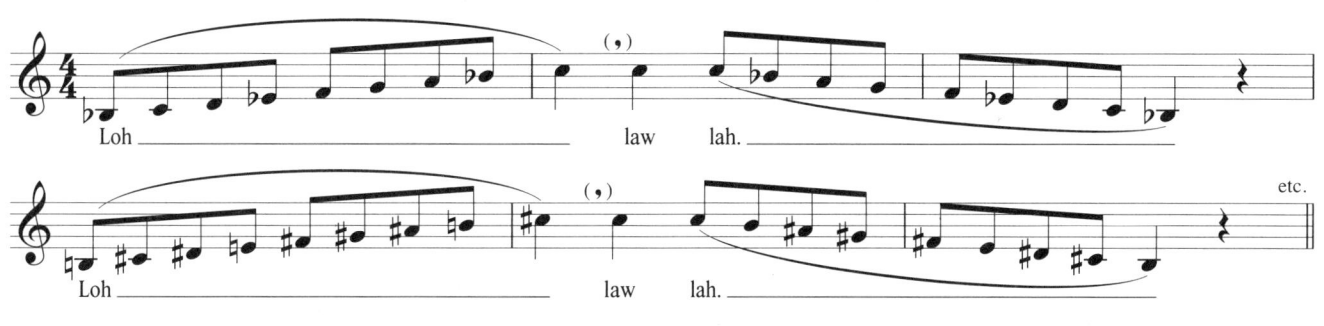

SAT

Topics: Nine-note scale; articulation; breath management

Yesterday, we sang nine-note scales. Let's revisit that pattern, but add different rhythmic patterns and articulations. Use your support muscles on the staccato pitches and sing all the slurred notes legato. You'll want to practice this aerobic slowly at first, catching breaths as needed after the staccato notes. Increase the tempo only when you can sing the 16ths evenly, and work toward singing all four bars in a single breath.

SUN

Topics: Minor key; sixths; 16th notes; quick breaths

Sing this F-minor melody slowly, breathing as indicated. It may prove a challenge at first, but ultimately it is not hard as it looks. (Listen to the demo.) Notice that there are several upward leaps of a sixth, quite an expressive interval when handled with sensitivity. There are no syllables, no dynamic marks, no slurs. We're leaving this one to your musicality and imagination!

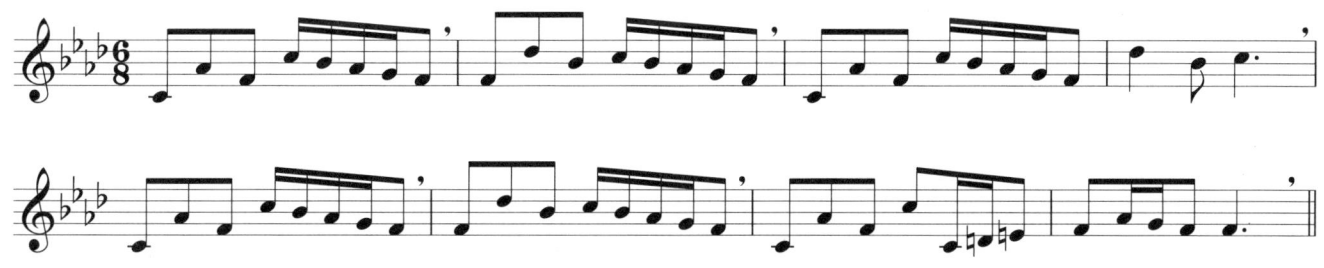

VOCAL AEROBICS — WEEK 37

MON

Topics: Five-note scales; nine-note scales; flexibility

At first glance, this exercise might look a bit complex. Break it down, though, and you'll see that we're merely combining five-note and nine-note scales. No syllables are indicated, so make use of the etude as best suits your needs. Some suggestions: 1) sing each note on a separate syllable, such as *bim* or *tah*; 2) use a hum and/or a tip trill; 3) use a variety of vowels, prefacing each note with *n* or *t*; 4) use a variety of vowels, singing each five-bar iteration on a single vowel.

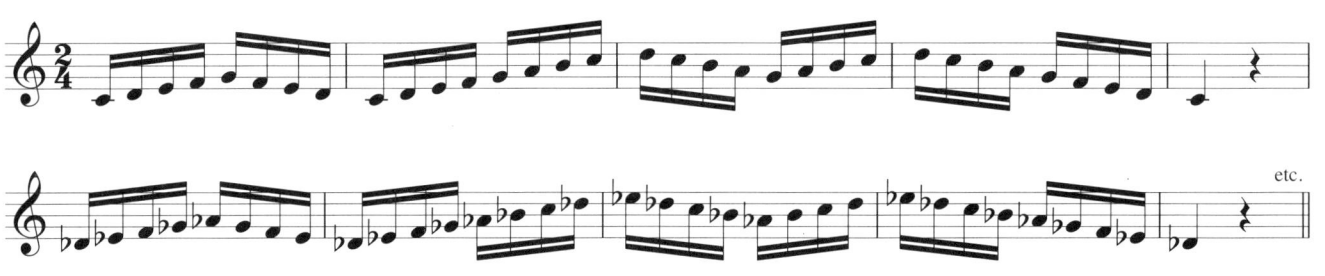

TUE

Topics: Familiar scale patterns; flexibility; range

Here, you'll find a combination of several familiar patterns: three-note scale, five-note scale, and six-note scale. Sing each four-bar phrase in a single breath on a single vowel sound, as shown. That's your final goal, at least. Begin slowly, though, breathing when you need to. Make sure the pitches are accurate by singing *tay* on each note. Over time, add vowel sounds. This is a good aerobic for vocal agility and for increasing your range.

WED

Topics: Diminution; half-steps

The melodic pattern here should look familiar. Last Thursday, we used it to practice *augmentation*. Now we'll use it to show *diminution*, in which the note values become progressively shorter. Make sure the half-step in bar 1 is well-tuned; that will help you when it recurs more quickly in bar 2. Sing this useful little aerobic across your entire range.

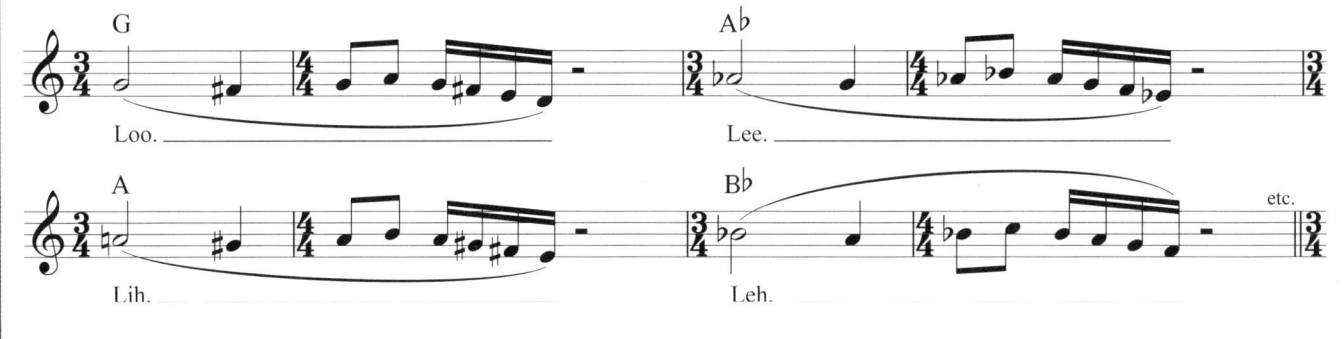

THU

Topics: Vocal strength; pitch accuracy; rhythmic acuity

We can reconfigure the five-note major scale to create a new pattern. Use your fast air to leap up the fifth on beat 2, then crescendo across the quarter note that follows. Aim to keep the tone full and strong as you descend, and make sure the 16th-notes are accurate in terms of rhythm and pitch.

FRI

Topics: Vocal strength; rhythm; range extension

There are three big dotted-quarter-note beats in 9/8 meter. Crescendo across the two pick-up notes and give a slight accent to the *-lu-* syllable. Keep the sound forte throughout, offsetting the natural tendency to get softer on the descending arpeggio. This is a great aerobic for building vocal strength and for extending your range. Sing it as high and as low as you comfortably can. Hallelujah!

SAT

Topics: Flexibility; breath management

Flexibility and breath management are our goals here. We want to be able to move the voice quickly and evenly across a string of 16th notes, letting them ride gently on our breath. Begin by singing a whole step on the first two beats of each pattern, then move up the five-note major scale and back down again. You'll notice there's a built-in crescendo as you ascend and a built-in diminuendo as you descend. Adjust your breath speed accordingly (faster going up…). It's a good idea to begin with closed vowels, as shown below. As you become more proficient, by all means practice with other vowel sounds.

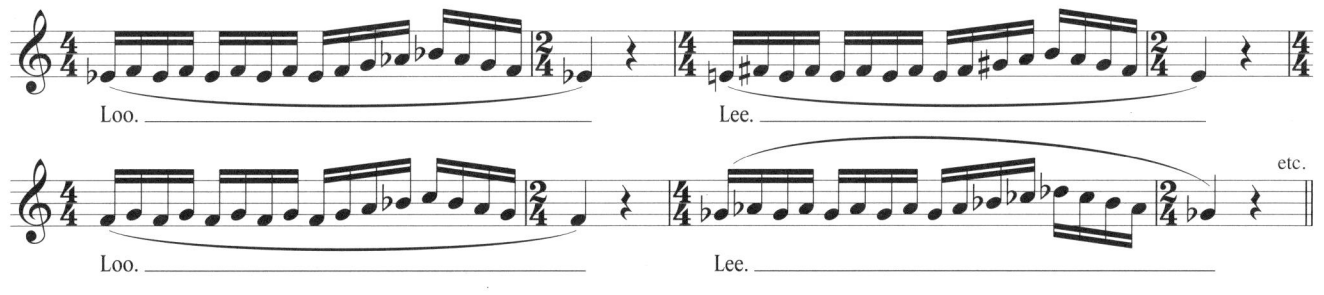

SUN

Topics: Range extension; flexibility; minor mode

Range extension, flexibility, and singing pitches accurately in the minor mode are our goals today. You'll notice that each iteration covers and octave plus a minor third. In bar 2, beware of the two even eighth notes that contrast with the triplet rhythm. The vowels become progressively more closed as you descend the pattern. You might need to listen to the demo track a couple of times to get the melody into your ears.

77

VOCAL AEROBICS — WEEK 38

MON

Topics: Vocal strength; breath management; intonation

Today's aerobic is similar to one we saw in Week 36. Re-read the instructions there and practice the exercise before beginning this one. You'll notice that things are a bit more advanced here: We're leaping an octave instead of a fifth; we're sustaining a whole-note instead of a half-note; we're descending an octave scale instead of a five-note scale. This is a great exercise for improving your breath management, increasing your vocal strength, and testing your pitch accuracy. Have fun—but listen to the demo first!

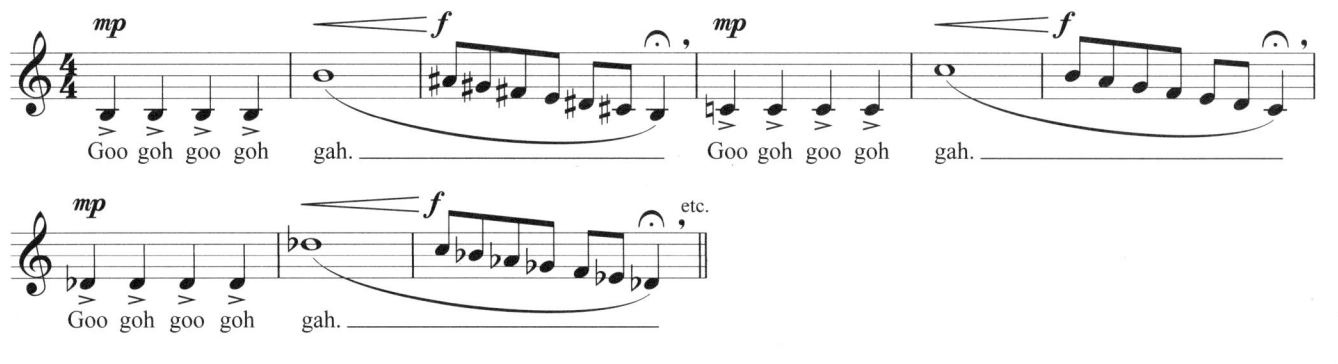

TUE

Topic: Descending chromatic scales

This time-worn exercise presents a real challenge. What we have here are descending chromatic scales across an octave. That means we're going to sing every discrete half step—every white and black note on the piano—from, say, one D to the D an octave lower. We have included no syllables on the printed example. It is helpful, in the first stages, to sing a separate syllable (try *tee*) on each note. To begin, you probably will want to play the notes on a keyboard as you descend. Over time, the goal is to sing all 13 notes on a single vowel, molto legato. Be patient with yourself on this one. It's instructive both for your ears and for your voice. Only the brave need apply.

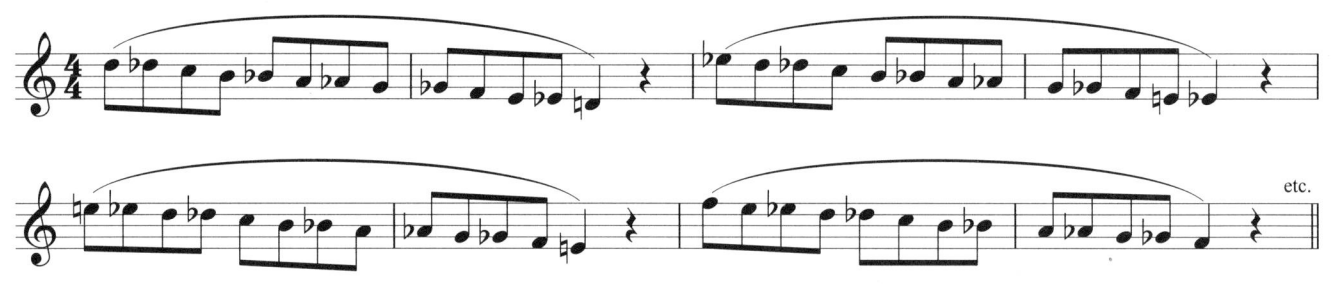

WED

Topic: Nine-note scale, descending/ascending

This nine-note scale should look familiar. Take a look at Saturday in Week 36 and you'll notice that we've flipped it upside-down. Singing down/up is a different physical sensation than singing up/down. Let's explore by first singing the earlier etude, then this one. Use the initial *h* consonant and the staccato eighth note to launch you into a firm start. Strive for a forte sound throughout, and aim to sing all four bars with only one inhalation.

THU

Topics: Agility; range extension

Let's work on agility and range extension. The ascending arpeggio here outlines the tonic (I) chord, while the descending one limns the dominant-seventh (V7) chord. Use a metronome to practice at various tempos, beginning slowly and eventually moving up to super-fast. Use the vowels indicated here, then mix and match syllables of your own creation.

FRI

Topics: Repeated notes; two-note phrases; upward leaps; expressivity

As you tackle the technical aspects of this etude—with its two-note phrases and repeated pitches—remember that those same aspects lend it the potential for expressive singing. (You already know to lean into the first note and ease off on the second.) Give shape to the larger phrases as well. You'll notice that the key signature indicates D major and that the chord progression is one of the most common ever, I-vi-ii-V7-I.

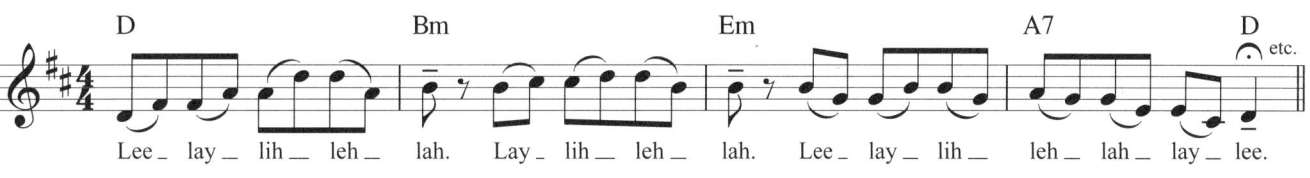

SAT

Topics: Flexibility; intonation; breath management

Nine-notes scales are a great way to get the voice moving flexibly over a wider range of pitches. Here, we have an eight-note (octave) major scale, plus the note above it. Start slowly at first, but at a tempo that allows you to sing two-bar phrases in a single breath. You can ensure better pitch accuracy if you begin by singing a single syllable (*bim*, for example) on each 16th note. As you become more proficient, sing a single vowel sound across the phrase. As always, beware of the half steps. No syllables are given in the music example below. It's your choice!

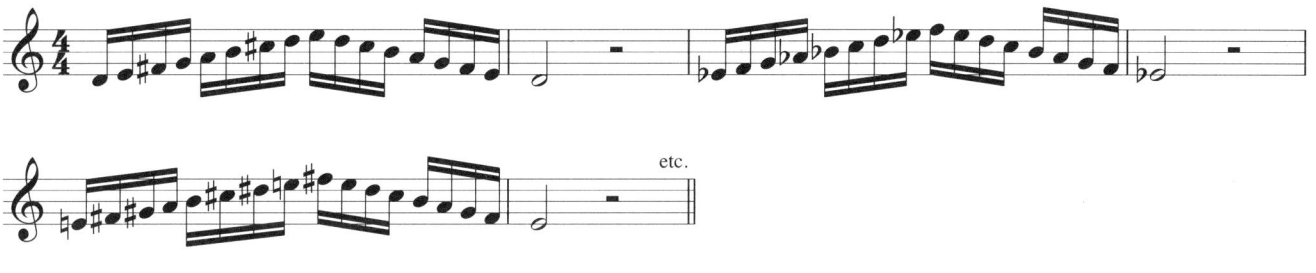

SUN

Topics: Range extension; legato

Today's aerobic is a bit advanced. It requires the range of an octave plus a fifth. That's what's called for to sing "The Star-Spangled Banner," high notes and all, so you know it's a challenge! On the first two beats, we're singing a broken tonic (I) chord; on beats 3 and 4, we sing a broken dominant-seventh (V7) chord. Sing molto legato and give shape to the phrase—up, over, and back down again. As always, when you've reached your topmost comfortable note, stop. We've indicated an *ah* vowel, but add others of your choosing as well.

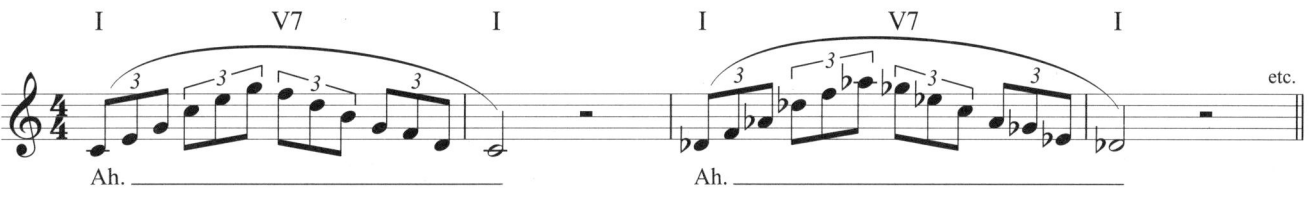

VOCAL AEROBICS — WEEK 39

MON
Topic: Octave chromatic scale
In Week 33, we practiced the chromatic scale using quarter notes, singing a syllable on each one. Now let's employ eighth notes and a single vowel sound. Start slowly at first, to make sure you stay in tune. Use your keyboard to help. Over time, increase the tempo, and sing *a cappella*. Keep the vowel sounds pure and use good breath support.

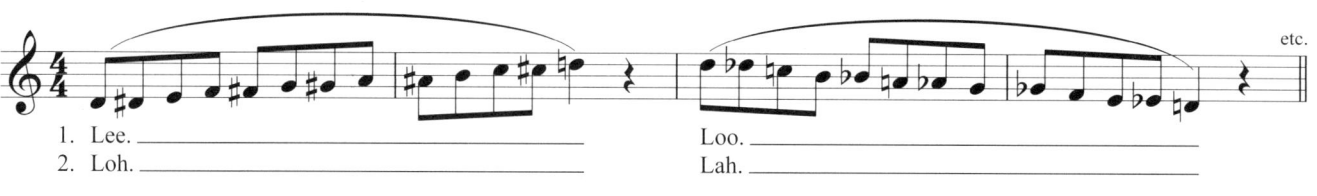

1. Lee. Loo.
2. Loh. Lah.

TUE
Topic: Dorian mode
In addition to the familiar major (Ionian) and minor (Aeolian) modes, there are five others that date back to the Middle Ages. One of the most common of these is the Dorian mode. On your keyboard, play from D up to the next D, sounding only the white notes. That's the Dorian scale. It's like the natural minor (from A to A on your keyboard), except that the sixth note is raised a half-step. Pop songs set in this mode include The Beatles' "Eleanor Rigby," Jimi Hendrix's "Purple Haze," Chris Isaak's "Wicked Game," and the one shown below. Simon and Garfunkel combined an original melody with this traditional English folksong to create "Scarborough Fair/Canticle." Find an online performance—and listen to the demo track, too.

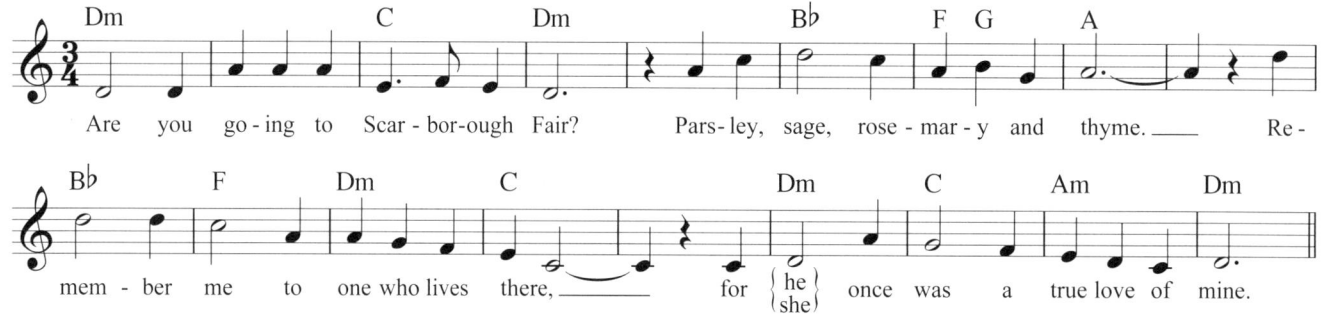

WED
Topics: Flexibility; range extension
This jaunty aerobic takes the octave major scale—ascending and descending—as its skeleton. We're singing skips and steps in a triplet configuration to improve our agility and increase our vocal range. Listen to the demo track. Eventually, you'll want to sing it that way, in two big, fast phrases. To get there, slow it down and use the practice tools discussed earlier in the book.

Moh. Mah.

THU

Topic: Syncopation

We're keeping the melody (and harmony) simple here, because we want to focus on performing the syncopated rhythms accurately. Before you even sing the etude, practice by clapping a steady quarter-note rhythm and speaking the syllables in the correct place. (You'll notice that quite a few notes occur on the offbeats—that's what syncopation is, after all!) Use the syllables given below, then make up your own. It's fun!

FRI

Topic: Pitch accuracy

In the music of every style and every era, one of the most commonly encountered intervals is the fourth from *sol* (the fifth of the scale) up to *do* (the root note). The familiar tune below comes from Mozart's *Eine kleine Nachtmusik* (A Little Night Music). It's a great mnemonic device to practice that interval. You'll notice that the first two bars outline the tonic (I) chord, while bars 3 and 4 limn the dominant-seventh (V7) chord. Sing the *solfège* syllables as marked, then make up your own.

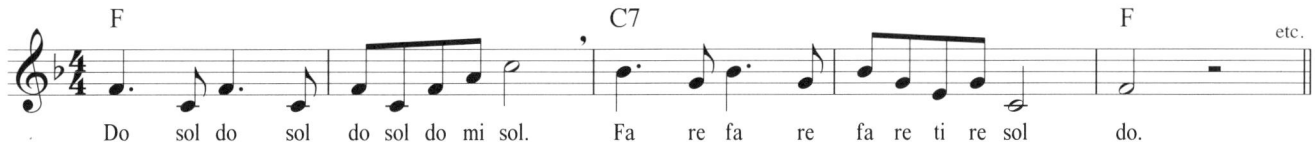

SAT

Topics: Facility; breath management; range extension

Look at the music example below. This etude combines the five-note scale with the nine-note scale, using 16th notes. It is a good workout for vocal facility, for breath management, and for range extension. You will need to practice over several days and weeks. At first, choose a moderate tempo that allows accuracy, singing *dee* on each note. When that becomes second nature, revert to a slower tempo, singing only a single *dee* across the two-bar phrase. Ultimately, you should breathe only on the quarter rests.

SUN

Topics: Dynamics; phrase shape

Cast your gaze upon the masterpiece below. It is completely devoid any expressive markings; you are tasked with supplying them. The online demo is only one option of many, so try it several ways. Remember that I (*ah-ee*) is a diphthong, so sustain the primary vowel as long as you can; use it again for lahv. For *sing*, keep height in the *ih* vowel and review the *ng* etude in week 13. Don't you just love these little ditties?

VOCAL AEROBICS
WEEK 40

Here we are at the last week of *Vocal Aerobics*. As with any acquired skill, singing is a lifelong pursuit. It requires regular practice, and we never stop learning how to sing better and more healthily. Obviously, this book was never intended as a "once through, then done" enterprise. You can use the etudes in this book for as long as you continue singing, mixing them up as you see fit.

"I Ain't Got Nobody (And Nobody Cares for Me)" was first published in 1915—the time of vaudeville, Tin Pan Alley, and World War I. With lyrics by Roger Graham and music by Spencer Williams and Dave Peyton, over the following generations it became a well-known standard. Recorded in styles ranging from jazz to pop to country, the song was covered by the likes of Louis Armstrong, Rosemary Clooney, Louis Prima, Fats Waller, the Mills Brothers, and even David Lee Roth (of Van Halen fame).

Its signature opening phrase—a descending chromatic line—is unmistakable, and recurs several times. Let's practice this—first on noo, then with the words—moving down by half-steps to traverse a perfect fourth. Keep this well-tuned; it's easy to go flat. (The descending half-steps are a feature of the bridge, too!)

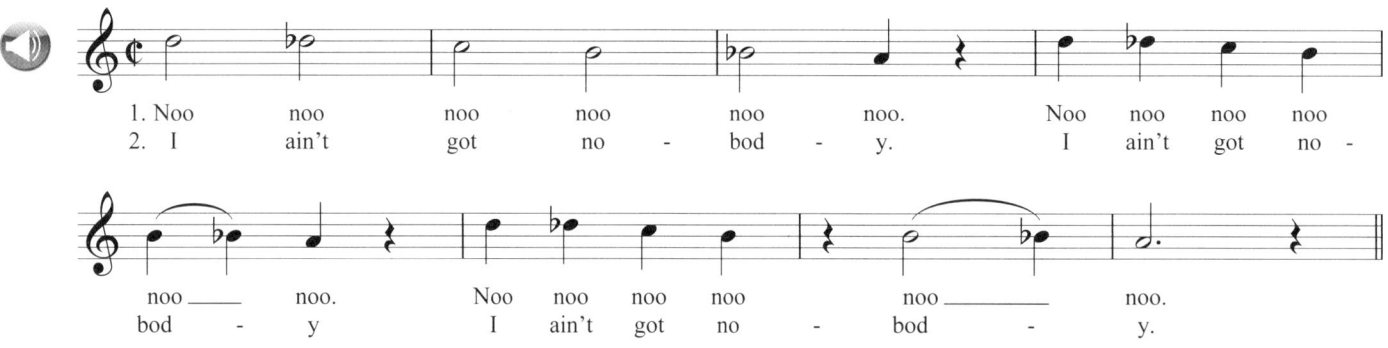

Notice that the song is set in cut-time, so you should feel two big half-note beats per bar. The syncopated rhythms that occur on the second half of several measures have more pizzazz if you accent the short note and ease off the longer note. Give it a try, initially with some "scat" syllables—use these and/or make up your own—then with several short phrases from the song's lyrics.

The sheet music on the following page is in G major, as are the demo and backing tracks. If this feels a little high for you altos and baritones, use the transposing feature to find a key that is comfortable for you. Have fun!

ACKNOWLEDGMENTS

Decades of choral rehearsals and voice lessons – variously as student, teacher, and accompanist – fueled the ideas for the exercises found in *Vocal Aerobics*. Proper attribution would therefore be impossible. The names are far too many, and some likely forgotten. I owe a debt of gratitude that I cannot properly acknowledge.

I am grateful to Jeff Schroedl for offering the opportunity to author this book, and to the many people at Hal Leonard LLC for making it a reality – particularly Kimberly Brand, Nicole Julius, Jennifer Schmidt, and Matthew Wolf. Thank you so much for your help.

Finally, I owe a special thanks to my wife, Susan Loris, the best and smartest person I know. Her support and encouragement kept me going on those days when writing one more etude felt like a Sisyphean task.

ABOUT THE AUTHOR

J. Mark Baker is the founding director of Milwaukee Chamber Choir, a professional-level ensemble of 28 singers. An experienced choral conductor, singer, and music educator, he holds a doctorate in choral music from the University of Illinois at Urbana-Champaign. As a professional member of the Chicago Symphony Chorus, Dr. Baker sang under the direction of today's leading conductors and was a recipient of the CSC's Margaret Hillis Foundation scholarship for continuing vocal studies. He has sung in Europe, in Canada, and at Carnegie Hall.

A church musician for over 30 years, he has served congregations in four states in a variety of roles: choirmaster, organist, section leader/soloist. As a music editor, he has prepared a five-volume *Anthology of Italian Opera*, a four-volume set of Mozart opera arias, and the collected songs of Maurice Ravel, as well as choral music by Debussy, Duruflé, Poulenc, Ravel, and Respighi. Dr. Baker is the program annotator for the Milwaukee Symphony Orchestra.

A native of Alabama, Dr. Baker holds a Bachelor of Music degree from the University of Montevallo and a Master of Music degree from Illinois State University.

ABOUT THE ONLINE AUDIO

The price of this book includes access to online audio, for download or streaming, using the unique code on the title page. Including PLAYBACK+, a multi-functional audio player that allows you to slow down audio without changing pitch, set loop points, change keys, and pan left or right – available exclusively from Hal Leonard. When using the backing tracks, make use of these features to find the key and tempo that work best for you.

Vocals: Jesse Weinberg & Rebecca Whitney

Piano: J. Mark Baker

Recording engineer: Ric Probst

Recorded at Tanner-Monagle Studios; Milwaukee, WI